1985

KINGS AND QUEENS
OF ENGLAND

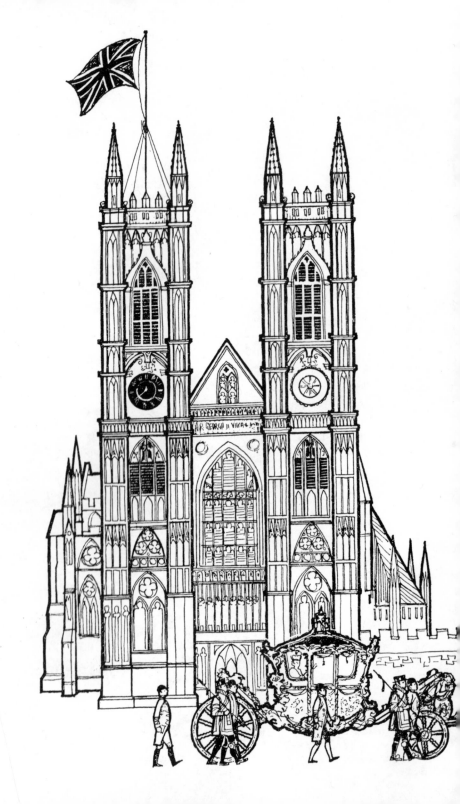

KINGS and QUEENS
of ENGLAND

[with 32 Portraits in Color]

M. C. SCOTT MONCRIEFF

Including an Essay on
ROYAL PORTRAITURE
by Richard Ormond
Assistant Keeper, National Portrait Gallery

BLANDFORD PRESS
POOLE   DORSET

© 1966 BLANDFORD PRESS LTD
Link House, West Street, Poole, Dorset BH15 1LL

First published 1966
Reprinted 1969
Revised Edition 1973
Reprinted 1978

ISBN 0 7137 06635

Printed in Great Britain by Fletcher & Son Ltd, Norwich

CONTENTS

ROYAL PORTRAITS
LIST OF ILLUSTRATIONS

6

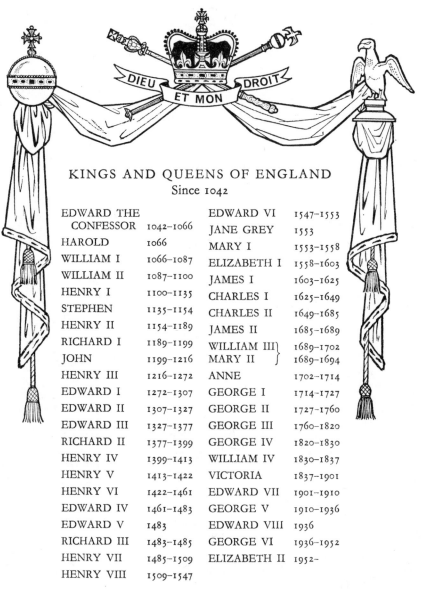

KINGS AND QUEENS OF ENGLAND
Since 1042

EDWARD THE CONFESSOR	1042–1066	EDWARD VI	1547–1553
		JANE GREY	1553
HAROLD	1066	MARY I	1553–1558
WILLIAM I	1066–1087	ELIZABETH I	1558–1603
WILLIAM II	1087–1100	JAMES I	1603–1625
HENRY I	1100–1135	CHARLES I	1625–1649
STEPHEN	1135–1154	CHARLES II	1649–1685
HENRY II	1154–1189	JAMES II	1685–1689
RICHARD I	1189–1199	WILLIAM III	1689–1702
JOHN	1199–1216	MARY II	1689–1694
HENRY III	1216–1272	ANNE	1702–1714
EDWARD I	1272–1307	GEORGE I	1714–1727
EDWARD II	1307–1327	GEORGE II	1727–1760
EDWARD III	1327–1377	GEORGE III	1760–1820
RICHARD II	1377–1399	GEORGE IV	1820–1830
HENRY IV	1399–1413	WILLIAM IV	1830–1837
HENRY V	1413–1422	VICTORIA	1837–1901
HENRY VI	1422–1461	EDWARD VII	1901–1910
EDWARD IV	1461–1483	GEORGE V	1910–1936
EDWARD V	1483	EDWARD VIII	1936
RICHARD III	1483–1485	GEORGE VI	1936–1952
HENRY VII	1485–1509	ELIZABETH II	1952–
HENRY VIII	1509–1547		

INTRODUCTION

The Royal Crown of England, symbol of monarchy, is guarded in London's ancient fortress, the Tower.

Of the many thousands of visitors who come to view it, some may remember the day when the present Queen wore it at her coronation in 1953. The Great Crown (called St Edward's) weighs nearly five pounds and was only worn for a short time in the ceremony because it is so heavy; then it was changed for a lighter one. The Queen also carried the orb and sceptre, and wore the bracelets on her arms. A tiny golden flask shaped like an eagle contains oil, and from its open beak came the drop to anoint her forehead. These can all be seen in the Tower.

Purple velvet, pure gold, a rim of black and white ermine, pearls, precious stones—the crown, though heavy to wear, is lovely to look at, and designed to be viewed from all sides. "To be a King and wear a Crown," remarked one of Her Majesty's predecessors, Queen Elizabeth I, "is a thing more glorious to them that see it than it is pleasant to them that bear it."

This book tells something of the men and women who have worn England's Crown in the past. Not all of them wore this actual one, but all had the right to be crowned. Some of their reigns were short and full of strife, while others were relatively peaceful. Jane Grey had a nine days' reign, and Edward V less than two months, but Victoria was Queen for almost sixty-four years.

From the Tower beside the Thames, where the stately diadem reposes, it is only a short distance, some two miles upstream, to the place where so many vivid scenes in English history were enacted, and where sovereigns are crowned: Westminster Abbey.

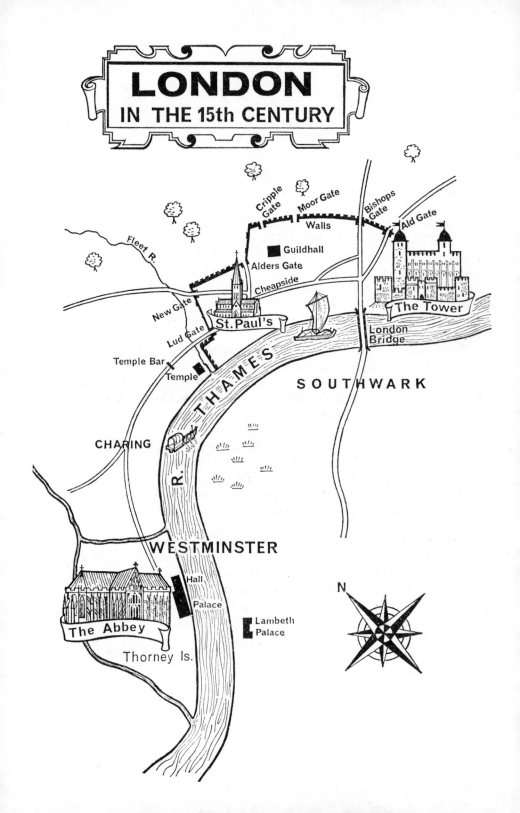

CHAPTER ONE

Edward the Confessor: Harold

I

Long before the Embankment was made, the Thames followed its irregular course among mudbanks and marshes, islets and meadows, gradually widening out to its estuary and the sea.

At one place west of what is now the City of London, a tributary stream on the north side branched into two before joining the river, and thus formed a small island, on which brambles and hawthorns grew. It was called Thorney.

The Romans who conquered southern Britain in the first century built a soldiers' camp on this island, and also raised a temple to Apollo the sun-god. Nobody knows how long the Apollo-worship continued, but after the Roman legions left Britain the place was neglected, the stream gradually filled in, the marshes dried and Thorney was no longer surrounded by water. Some time later, Christian monks were known to be living on the firm ground of the island site; they worshipped God there in a small simple church, probably built of wood.

London was not yet England's capital, nor was there yet an England in the sense that is usually understood. Instead, there were several smaller kingdoms: London lay between those of the East, Middle and South Saxons (Essex, Middlesex and Sussex) and the kingdom of Kent. Winchester was where the kings of Wessex, or the West Saxons, most often wore their crowns. The Saxon king who chose Thorney as a site to build, both a palace for himself and a new and larger church, was Edward the Confessor.

2

One of Edward's forefathers was the wise and valiant King Alfred of Wessex; but his own father was a feeble king who let the Danes overrun Wessex and the other kingdoms, and conquer them. Edward was a child at that time. His mother fled with him over the sea to Normandy, where Edward lived and was educated.

French was spoken in Normandy, though the land-owners were

descended from Norse and Danish sea-rovers. The Normans were a hardy race, accustomed to travelling, hunting and fighting on horseback. They were good builders, too, and used their local stone in a style simple and massive, yet not without some vivid ornament.

Like Normandy, England was the home of mixed races, but her Angles, Saxons and Danes were slowly merging into one folk, to whom the Normans with their French tongue were strangers.

When Edward became King of England he was crowned first at Canterbury, then at Winchester. A child no longer, but a middle-aged man, he had plump pink cheeks, and hair and beard so fair as to look white. His manners were so gentle and dignified and his habits of prayer and church-going so diligent, that he was given the rank of "confessor" which is one of the steps towards sainthood. (Long after his lifetime he was canonised.)

A bodyguard of Norman knights came over with Edward, and French was always spoken at his court. Among the royal servants, Normans soon began to gain favours and promotions. The King's cousin Duke William of Normandy visited him in state. Edward's partiality to these foreign incomers irritated the Saxons, but he took little notice. In the following years a Saxon earl named Godwin tried hard to oust the Normans, and to raise his own and his family's fortunes. Edward, who had married Godwin's daughter Edith, refused to quarrel. What interested him far more was the enrichment and founding of churches.

He was especially keen to build a new minster (monastery church) to replace the small one on the Thorney site west of London. It was to resemble the many abbeys Edward had seen in Normandy with their thick walls, strong supporting columns and round-arched windows. Plans were therefore drawn up, and Norman masons started on the foundations. Aided by less skilled Saxon workmen they raised the minster walls, using blocks of white stone quarried at Reigate. A tenth of the King's income was set aside for the work, year after year.

The palace also was begun, on a site nearer the river, and was finished first. The minster, which took fifteen years to build, was to be ready by the end of A.D. 1065. But as Christmas of that year approached, the King became ill, and grew worse; and as he seemed unlikely to recover, people wondered who would succeed to the throne if he should die.

To become king, a man had to be elected by the Witan, or Council of

Wise Men, who usually chose the former king's eldest son. But Edward was childless.

There were three possible successors:

1. Edward's great-nephew, *Edgar*. He belonged to the royal family, but was young (15) and not very forceful.

2. Edward's brother-in-law, *Harold*. Son of the Saxon Earl Godwin and of a Danish mother, Harold, aged 43, tall and active, owned land in sixteen English counties and could command their fighting men.

3. Edward's cousin, *William*, Duke of Normandy, aged 38. Edward had named him as the heir, but had only spoken, not written, his wish.

The Norman duke also declared that Harold had sworn to help him (William) to gain the English crown. Harold, however, protested that he had been forced to swear it, and under false pretences. Clearly, then, the question would only be settled by some test of strength between these last two, Saxon Harold and Norman William.

Such thoughts must have been uppermost in many minds when, on December 28th, 1065, the Abbey of the West Minster was dedicated with due ceremony "to the honour of God and St Peter". King Edward could not be present. He was lying on his death-bed in the palace across the way. As he gloomily foretold a stormy year for the kingdom, his voice could hardly be heard; his cheeks were pale and his hands were so thin that the light could be seen through them. Queen Edith sat at his feet.

On January 5th, 1066, he died.

The Witan had made up their minds; they knew which man England wanted as king. Harold was chosen.

EDWARD THE CONFESSOR
From an engraving by John Smith
of the altar window, Rumford Church

KING EDWARD THE CONFESSOR'S
SHRINE IN WESTMINSTER ABBEY

3

Harold lost no time and was crowned in the new Abbey the very next day. Then he rode up to York, about 190 miles, to make sure he was accepted as king in the country north of the Humber. Having satisfied himself on that point, he was back at Westminster in time for Easter.

Although Saxons and Danes were becoming one people, England still was far from united. The earls in the midlands and north proved to be more intent on keeping what power they had than on helping Harold to defend the country from external dangers. They either helped him grudgingly or not at all. Harold's own family were not united either: out of his five brothers the sons of Godwin, only two—Gyrth and Leofwin—could be counted upon as loyal supporters, while another one, Tostig, turned out to be a traitor.

During the spring of 1066 William of Normandy was busy preparing to invade England and make good his claim to its crown. Harold kept a fleet, mostly fishing vessels, guarding the south coast, and an army was on the watch, but after four months he could not afford to maintain them any longer. He laid up the ships and let the men go home.

Tostig, who had quarrelled with his royal brother and gone abroad to make trouble, chose this moment to strike. With the King of Norway and 300 ships full of Norwegian warriors, Tostig landed in Yorkshire, beat off all attempts to stop him, and captured York. On hearing of this disaster Harold prayed all night at Waltham, an abbey he had founded near London. He then quickly recalled his disbanded army and led them northwards. In battle at Stamford Bridge both Tostig and the Norwegian king were defeated and killed. Those Norwegians left alive retreated to their ships and went home.

While at York feasting to celebrate his victory, Harold was told that his enemy from Normandy had struck. William and an invading force had landed on the Sussex coast. Not a moment was to be lost, and after sending out a summons to every available man through the shires of England to meet him in London, Harold set off again.

With men already tired after the recent marching and fighting, he accomplished the extraordinary feat of reaching London in five days. Two northern earls who were supposed to be coming to join him were left far behind; but they would have been of little use, as they were half-hearted, and they finally left him alone. Gyrth advised Harold to go at a slower pace and let the Normans come further into England—to them, a country of enemies—but Harold, eager to get to grips with his rival, disregarded his brother's advice.

Barely a fortnight after leaving York, he had taken up his position on a ridge above Hastings where the Normans were encamped. The great forest of the Weald behind them gave some shelter to Harold's troops, who slept the night there, wearily as may be imagined.

4

The adventurers from Normandy had had a fortnight on this side of the sea to prepare themselves for battle, and were fresh and fit. From early next morning until sunset (October 14th) the two armies fought with scarcely a pause. Their day-long struggle is now called the Battle of Hastings. As we can see now, it was to decide not merely which man should inherit King Edward's crown, but what England's own future was to be: either a self-contained little plot of Anglo-Saxondom or a part of the main stream of European life, thought and culture.

Even if no one then regarded the battle in that way, William must have known that for him the whole invasion was a gamble. He had staked everything on the death or capture of his Saxon rival and his own acceptance by the Witan.

First his cavalry attacked the main Saxon body up on the ridge. Naturally horses weighed down with men and armour can charge more easily downhill than up—which Harold may have had in mind when choosing his position. The Saxons stood firm, shoulder to shoulder and shield to shield, behind a trench and stockade. They could not be dislodged.

Seeing his mounted knights fail, William narrowed down his own field of action and aimed at the spot where Harold stood, surrounded by a bodyguard and marked out by two painted standards, the Dragon of Wessex and the Golden Man. William, along with his half-brothers Odo and Robert—Bishop of Bayeux and Count of Mortain—reached Harold who stood with his brothers Gyrth and Leofwin. It was three against three, although the fighting around them did not slacken.

William killed Gyrth with one swing of his terrible spiked club. Leofwin fell dead from another Norman blow. But Harold, who was strong enough to hew down a rider and horse in one sword-stroke, kept out of his enemy's reach.

William was resourceful and had spent much of his life mastering difficulties. He next tried a ruse; his men feigned to retreat and the

Saxons nearest rushed down after them, leaving their own centre un-
defended. Yet even then Harold kept control, though now he was
exposed to attack from different directions; the day was lengthening, it
was afternoon, and still for three mortal hours against the impetus and
discipline of the Norman cavalry he doggedly fought on.

Finally at sunset William massed all his archers in front, and although accurate aim was impossible in the dusk he ordered them to
shoot up towards the Saxon centre. A shower of arrows hissed through
the air. One of them hit Harold's right eye, and he collapsed. Twenty
Norman knights, who had all vowed to capture his standard, charged
in; most of them were killed, but four fell upon the dying King and
savagely ended his life. His remaining followers scattered and fled into
the forest.

Next day Harold was buried on the sea-shore at Pevensey, though his
body was removed later to his abbey at Waltham. An abbey was built
also over the spot where this valiant defender of his kingdom had been
struck down. It was called, quite simply, Battle Abbey.

If ever a battle was hard fought, that one was, and if ever a battle
deserved to be remembered, that one did.

BATTLE ABBEY
Fourteenth-century gatehouse

CHAPTER TWO

William I

I

A coronation consists of much more than the actual placing of the crown. Three other essential parts of the ceremony come first.

To begin with, the people shout aloud to show they approve of the choice that has been made. Nowadays the Westminster scholars do the shouting. "Vivat rex!" they say for a king, or "Vivat regina!" meaning "Long live the Queen!"

Next, the threefold oath: the sovereign swears to protect the Church, to promote justice and punish evildoers. So, with varying words but the same intention, have all the kings sworn since long before Edward the Confessor's time.

Third, the anointing: the sovereign is touched with oil, the outward sign of God's grace.

Only after all this has been done, is the climax reached; ring, sword and sceptre are given and the crown is put on.

Two and a half months after his victory at Hastings Duke William was at Westminster, ready for his coronation. The Witan—scared, uneasy and not all of one mind—were most of them present. It had seemed best to elect William when he asked for it. Young Edgar stood among them. William wanted to be regarded as the Confessor's lawful heir, and therefore chose the Abbey, so closely connected with Edward, as the place of his crowning; while he timed it for Christmas, because on that day the Saxon kings had been accustomed to wear their crowns and feast in state.

The service was to be exactly the same as in times past. William, "fierce, huge and unwieldy", as Dean Stanley describes him, stood there facing the Archbishop of York, the clergy and monks and a full congregation, both Saxon and Norman. A mixed crowd waited outside, watched by William's mounted guards.

The ceremony began, but soon took an unexpected turn. The Archbishop invited the Saxons present to shout in the usual way for William; a Norman bishop speaking in French did the same to the Normans, for

B   17

neither people understood each other's language. The answer was a deafening roar in both languages. It sounded so threatening that the guards outside the Abbey thought a riot had begun.

In the midst of the clamour, flames were seen shooting up from the abbey gate and the thatched wooden buildings close by, and cries of "Fire, fire!" added to the din. If a house caught fire in those days, people would automatically rush to put the blaze out or, maybe, help themselves to what loot they could find in the confusion. In a few moments the entire congregation, Witan and all, had disappeared from the sacred building. The excitement and noise outside raged back and forth until the fires died down, and in the early darkness of a midwinter afternoon the crowd dispersed.

Within, William and the clergy, though startled, had remained still; then the Archbishop continued in a low voice where he had left off. The moment of crowning came, and the diadem (made by a French goldsmith) was duly set upon the Duke's head. There in the gloom of the cold, almost empty abbey, sat the huge man on his throne, King William of England, his ambition realised. There was no congratulation, no triumphal music, no voice of friend or foe; only a strange silence.

2

Shortly after Christmas William set men to work in the city of London, digging foundations at the eastern angle where the city's ancient wall met the river. Soon the Tower began to take shape; in his son's reign its white stones and corner turrets would be reflected in the Thames as they may be seen still.

Much had to happen, William knew, before he was king in reality as well as in name, because many parts of England were rebellious. The Tower was a visible sign of his strength. From those narrow windows his men could spy all round and see if armed Saxons were gathering to resist them. Within those twenty-foot-thick walls they themselves were safe and could overawe the city.

Strongholds like it were erected elsewhere for the same purpose. In south-west England where Harold's mother made a brave stand, the Norman castle at Exeter marked the end of her rebellion. In the northeast a "new castle" was built upon the river Tyne and so named the city that grew up round the walls. In between, castles of stone or wood on cliff or hillock marked the stopping-places of William's followers from Normandy, who were entrusted by him to hold the land that had been won. Such a landholder was called a baron or tenant-in-chief of the King, and the estate round his dwelling was called his fief.

It took four years and much bloodshed and destruction before William was fully "the Conqueror" of all England. Only once during that time did he feel confident enough to leave for a few months and attend to the affairs of Normandy, whose duke he still was. Later, back in England, he sent for Matilda his wife and their young sons Robert and William, and in 1068 Matilda was crowned as Queen. Their third son was born at Winchester, and named Henry.

3

All the land in England, cultivated or not, was owned by William. Corn, meat, milk, wool, leather, wood, everything necessary was brought in from the land. He and his court lived on the produce of those fiefs that he kept aside for his own use and did not grant away.

Some years after the Conquest he had a land-survey made, to make sure he was receiving all his dues. It was called Domesday Book. County by county it recorded how much was tilled and how much was waste or woodland; how many inhabitants there were, how many animals, mills, fishponds and many other details. The whole picture was drawn as it was in the year of the survey and also as it had been in Edward the Confessor's time, that is about twenty years earlier. Hence it could be seen whether the value had gone up or down. It can be deduced from the sharp fall in value of some estates which parts of the country had been plundered and devastated. The worst region was north of the Humber, where a broad belt of land was destroyed from coast to coast and took many generations to recover. William was merciless to rebels, and York was the last major city to oppose him in arms.

Domesday Book was meant to show him also what military manpower he could count upon, i.e. how many armed tenants could be called up, ready to check disorder in England and carry out his other commitments in Normandy.

One sore subject between William and the conquered people was his treatment of the forest areas. He loved hunting, and if a tract of land was declared a forest, so as to preserve the wild animals in it for him to hunt, the people living there came under special laws and might be evicted from their dwellings, whether they had another place to go to or not. But in general, and intentionally, William left the laws and customs unchanged. Sessions of justice formerly held in the shire courts continued there, as well as in the newer courts held by barons in their own castle or manor hall. He gave the London merchants a Charter allowing them to carry on business as formerly and had it written in the Saxon any of them could understand.

Alert as he was to all signs of unrest, William could feel secure in the support of bishops and clergy, and the knowledge that the Pope had blessed his enterprise. When the Primacy fell vacant William was able to fill it with a good friend already known to him in Normandy, Lanfranc of Pavia. As Archbishop of Canterbury Lanfranc proved a wise counsellor and made the transition from Saxon to Norman rule in the Church less troublesome than it might have been.

William's wife, who died a few years before him, was always loyally submissive, but he was too much of a dictator at home to arouse any affection in his sons. The elder two grew up unruly and boorish while the third, though better educated (and even able to speak Saxon as befitted one born in England), showed few signs of any but self-interested motives. The active dislike of all three for their father can be seen at the close of William's life.

A just though stern overlord to all his tenants-in-chief, William himself had an overlord, the King of France. Frequent bickerings between them flared up, at a time when William was not well, into a furious quarrel. Recovering enough to raid the French king's territory in the Seine valley, William set a town on fire, and when he rode up to inspect it afterwards, was badly injured when his horse happened to tread on hot ash and reared up in fright. William was taken to Rouen, Normandy's capital, and lingered for three weeks in severe pain. As death drew near, all three of his sons, who might decently have gathered around his bed, hastened away to seize their inheritances, and all his attendants deserted him, leaving the house stripped of everything movable. So the Conqueror passed away in an empty, gloomy silence that reminds one of his coronation: then he had been almost, now he was completely, alone.

CHAPTER THREE

William II: Henry I: Stephen

I

Robert, the eldest of the Conqueror's three sons, became Duke of Normandy. The second one, William (called Rufus because of his red colouring), inherited England's crown as William II. Castle-building continued, the Tower of London was completed, and William Rufus added a hall 240 feet long and 67½ feet wide to the palace of Westminster. It is still standing, although its present roof was put on later. Rufus, however, called the great hall a small bedroom, a mere trifle, compared with the size of the palace he was *going* to build. This, in spite of his boasting, he never did.

In order to win support from the Saxon people, Rufus promised to do away with the unpopular forest-laws made by his father. The Saxons believed him and sent armed men to fight for him as he asked. But the forest-laws were left unaltered. When Archbishop Lanfranc reminded him about them, Rufus demanded angrily, "Who can fulfil all his promises?" and did nothing further.

Empty words without action to follow do not win a man love and respect.

After Lanfranc's death, Rufus and his chief adviser used every means, fair and unfair, of filling the King's treasury; and the heavy taxes they imposed made them hated by Norman and Saxon alike.

Rufus was killed while out hunting in the New Forest. An arrow missed the stag it was aimed at and hit him instead. The man who shot the arrow—Walter Tyrrel—fled, as did every other man present, but afterwards he was believed not guilty. Some thought the shot was intentional, but nobody now can be sure.

At the King's funeral, no mass was sung; he was buried in silence.

2

Henry, the Conqueror's youngest son, had black hair falling over his brow, and eyes with a soft expression. This did not mean that his nature was soft.

Immediately on hearing of Rufus's death, Henry rode to Winchester and seized the King's treasury. Money might be needed, he thought, to pay men to fight for him to be king, as war between himself and his eldest brother seemed probable.

He was correct. Robert did claim the English crown. The two brothers clashed, first in argument and later in battle over in France. Henry won, imprisoned Robert for life and was called henceforward King Henry I of England and Duke of Normandy.

Henry was nearly as grasping as Rufus and tried every way he could to get money. His court had a special department dealing with the money which came in and that which was paid out. Clerks sat at a table measuring ten feet by five feet and covered with a chequered cloth like a chess-board. It helped them in their reckoning, to place the coins for one purpose on black squares, and for another purpose on coloured ones. The office was called The Court of the Exchequer, and even now, the royal servant or Minster responsible for our Queen's money is called Chancellor of the Exchequer.

Henry evidently did not want to be thought a bully and tyrant. At the outset he published the "Charter of Liberties", which was valid for the whole country, not merely for London. In it he renewed the promises made in his coronation oath. Some years later he gave London a Charter of its own as well. He sent judges from his court round the country; it reminded the people even in outlying districts that they had a king, and that he meant to protect them as well as needing their service.

Like Rufus, Henry had to face rebellion from some of his barons, but never let them get the upper hand. The King of Scots, too, had fought against Rufus, but Henry was on good terms with the Scots and married a Scottish princess; so there was peace on the Border and in Northern England.

Henry died of a fever brought on by over-eating. He had kept good order in the country, even though the strength in his character was mingled with hardness and greed.

3

A difficulty arose when Henry I died. His only son and heir had been drowned at sea, but he had a daughter, named Matilda. It was unusual then anywhere, and unheard of in England, that a woman should reign in her own right.

Most of the barons would not accept Matilda. They persuaded her cousin, Stephen of Blois (son of the Conqueror's daughter Adela, who had married a French count) to be crowned as king. Stephen was generally well liked.

Matilda who was proud and self-willed had looked upon herself as her father's heiress. Some barons took her part. Hence there was a long-drawn-out war—not for the sake of upholding any great idea, not even Normans against Saxons, but simply barons with their armed tenants, against other barons with theirs, each hoping to destroy their enemies' livelihood and to gain something out of it all for themselves.

The war might have been shortened if Stephen had been wiser and more determined. He was a mild man, they said, and no doer of justice. So the war dragged on, neither side being completely victorious, and a very wretched time it was.

At last the Archbishop of Canterbury persuaded the leaders to sign an agreement at Wallingford, and the fighting stopped. By this treaty, Stephen was taken by all to be the rightful king as long as he lived; but after his death, the crown was to go to Matilda's son, Henry of Anjou. Stephen only lived one more year after this, after a reign of nineteen years.

Those who refused to have a woman reigning over them, thus had the best of it; but a long civil war with all its suffering was a heavy price to pay.

CHAPTER FOUR

Henry II

I

Henry II, Matilda's son, was already Duke of Normandy and Count of Anjou. The Anjou family badge was a sprig of broom, and their name, derived from *planta genista* (broom-plant) was Plantagenet.

Henry was broad-shouldered and strong. A friend noticed him once going to greet someone at the far side of the room; there was a table between them and Henry vaulted over it instead of walking round. This little glimpse shows a man who was impulsive as well as energetic, and not much interested in kingly pomp and dignity. He had reddish hair, a freckled face with a heavy chin, and grey eyes that could blaze with anger. Few men were ever bold enough to cross Henry Plantagenet's will.

Through his wife Eleanor, who had inherited Aquitaine, he ruled over this huge Duchy which lay between the Loire and the Pyrenees—a distance roughly as long as England from Berwick down to Portsmouth. In course of time Henry made himself also overlord of Scotland, Ireland, Wales and Brittany, whose rulers did homage to him for their lands. All these dominions could be called an Empire, although that word was not actually used.

Henry's reign proved a far better time for England than Stephen's. The new King saw how much harm had resulted from the barons having no authority over them and each one doing as he liked.

The first royal orders were to pull down all castles that had been built without royal permission. Henry forbade barons to issue their own coinage: all money was to come from the royal mint. Former royal estates that other men had taken over were taken back by the King, and his own armed forces were made more efficient.

The plan started by Henry's grandfather (Henry I) of sending judges to travel through the country, was revived. They were sent once more on their rounds, so all districts were within reach of the King's justice. In each shire, the travelling judge would be met by groups of twelve men, who presented to him those accused of murder or robbery in their area. The twelve swore to say the truth (*quod illi verum dicent*) and give the facts they knew about the accused men, thus helping the judge to grasp what had happened, and award a suitable punishment, if any. It was far more effective than the old methods such as trial by ordeal, when the accused had to plunge his arm into boiling water and pick up a stone at the bottom of the cauldron; only if his skin healed within a week was he supposed to be innocent.

Meanwhile five judges sat on a bench in the King's own court and heard the pleas of men who had been wronged. The judgments given here became well known for being just—solidly based on what was right. In the manorial courts throughout the land, where barons heard complaints from their own tenants in their own hall, judgment was more apt to depend on personal fear or favour.

Henry II was well served by able men such as Theobald, the peace-making Archbishop who had secured the Treaty of Wallingford; Thomas Becket his secretary, to whom Henry gave the post of Chancellor; Ranulf Glanvill, expert in the laws; Bishop Nigel of Ely, the treasurer; and Richard de Lucy who acted for the King in England during his many absences abroad.

Henry trusted them and let them govern without interference. However, there was one exception, when one bold man dared to cross Henry Plantagenet's will.

2

The trouble began when Theobald, Archbishop of Canterbury, died and his place had to be filled.

Henry named for the post the man who was his best friend at the time, Chancellor Thomas Becket. The new Archbishop, who had been well known for his extravagance, now completely altered his way of living. Instead of spending largely on clothes and feasts and going out hunting with the King he fasted, wore a hair-shirt under his arch-bishop's robes and spent much time in study and prayer. On several minor matters he disagreed with the King, who grumbled, but gave way. Then came a major clash, when neither would give way.

It was on the question what should be done with clergy and clerks accused of crime. Who should sentence such a man to punishment, if he were found guilty? "A Church court," said Becket. "No, a royal court," said the King.

In the presence of the whole great Council, Becket defied the King.

25

Then, fearing for his life, the Archbishop fled abroad. He remained in France (not in Henry's part of it) for six years, while their case was discussed up and down Europe, the Pope and the King of France discreetly taking Becket's side, yet not daring to offend the mighty Plantagenet.

When Henry had his eldest son (also named Henry) crowned as King of England, so that the son would take his throne without hindrance when the father died, the coronation was performed by the Archbishop of York; and the young King's wife, Margaret, was not there to be crowned as Queen. The King of France, her father, furious at this neglect and discourtesy towards his daughter, asked the Pope to put England under an Interdict, which meant that the Church in England would become severed from Rome and be looked upon as outcast. In dread of such a threat being fulfilled, Henry went to see Becket in France, and gave him leave to return to England, but their interview was stiff and formal, neither having yielded one inch on the original subject of their quarrel.

On Becket's return to Canterbury he was joyfully greeted after his long absence. But two bishops, who had opposed him all along, refused to recognise him, and he excommunicated them. (This means much the same as an Interdict, but is used for a single person, not a whole country.)

On hearing what Becket had done, Henry flew into one of his rages, called the bystanders sluggards and shouted, "They let me be mocked by a low-born clerk!" Four knights who heard him hurried off to England, sought out the Archbishop and hacked him to death with their swords in Canterbury Cathedral.

Henry spent the rest of his life trying to prove that he had not meant Becket to be killed; but the deed was done. Very soon Becket was made a saint, and for centuries thousands of pilgrims came to visit his tomb.

It is little use arguing which of them was right in the quarrel. There was much to be said on Henry's side, because the royal courts of justice *were* proving themselves better than the Church courts, where too often the rascals among the clergy got off too easily. Yet Becket with his calm courage and his faithfulness to a higher Power than any king, towers above every other man in England at that time. He believed, in the words of St Peter, that "we ought to obey God rather than men".

3

During these years of conflict, naturally the other bishops and the barons had taken sides and the kingdom was very unsettled. Some barons were bent on regaining their power and rose in rebellion. One after another, Henry's sons, Henry, Richard and Geoffrey, rebelled also against their father. Their mother encouraged them; Henry kept her in prison. Only John, the youngest son, did not rebel.

Meanwhile the northern counties of England were invaded by Scots, and Henry, already in difficulties with his overlord the King of France, had to deal with crises in many places far apart. Here he showed his immense energy and determination. The rebels were overcome; the King of Scots was captured and forced to do homage for his kingdom. Henry seemed able to hold his own, and more.

His feelings as a father, however, can be imagined when his popular, handsome, troublesome but promising son, Henry, caught a fever and died. The old King who had grown more stubborn and irritable through the struggle with Becket, became even more bitter. He only lived a few more years. To the end of his life he was haunted by rebellions, and people said that Becket was having his revenge. The worst blow of all was to see the name of his youngest son John, whom he had loved most, heading the list of deserters and rebels.

Henry II deserves to be remembered not so much for his "Empire" which did not last long, nor even for the story of Becket, but for giving his lawyers and judges a chance to build processes of justice into the fabric of English life. England has a tradition of justice in which any Englishman can take pride. Trial by jury is established, and it means trusting to the honesty and common sense of ordinary people.

In his efforts to undo the barons' power, to limit the Church's power, and to build up the royal power, Henry had the backing of the lesser folk, and his methods proved workable. He had shown that the rule of force must give way to the rule of law.

CHAPTER FIVE

Richard I: John

I

Henry's second son Richard, already Duke of Aquitaine, who succeeded his father, only paid two visits to England, totalling six months, during his ten years' reign.

Before his father's death, Richard and other great lords in Europe had taken the Crusader's vow, to rescue Jerusalem which had been captured by the Turks under their famous leader Saladin. Hence Richard tended to regard England mainly as a piece of property from which, by taxes or other means, he could raise money for the Crusades.

He got it chiefly in large lump sums from the wealthier people. For instance, he sold the Archbishopric of York for £2,000. He put Ranulf Glanvill in prison, for no reason except that the old man was rich—King Henry's strong sense of justice not having descended to his sons—and this fetched a ransom of £15,000. The King of Scots bought back for 10,000 marks* his country's freedom; he had done homage to Henry II for it, and Richard, not specially wanting Scotland as his fief, was glad to take the cash instead.

With the proceeds of these and many similar bargains Richard left England and met King Philip Augustus of France at Vézelay. Together they rode away to the Holy War. With Richard also went Bishop Hubert Walter, and about 8,000 knights and foot-soldiers.

The two kings parted when they reached the south of France and Richard undertook two other wars, in Sicily and in Cyprus, before he reached the Holy Land. His wedding, which also took place in Cyprus, was splendidly celebrated, so altogether his expenses were heavy.

Richard married Princess Berengaria from Navarre. She was his mother's choice, as Queen Eleanor wanted Navarre, the neighbouring country to Aquitaine, to be an ally. Berengaria was intelligent though plain-looking, and Richard's good looks made up for her want of

---

* A mark was two-thirds of £1.

beauty; he was tall, with golden hair and blue eyes. But he could be cruel, and in later years he neglected her altogether.

In the Crusade, Richard "the Lionheart" won a high reputation. His chief enemy Saladin respected and admired him. Yet the enterprise failed, because the leaders of the European forces quarrelled. While Richard waited to attack Jerusalem he heard that his brother John had revolted against him—at home. The attempt to capture the Holy City was therefore given up, so that he could return to England without delay.

Delay there was, however. Richard was captured and imprisoned by the Duke of Austria during his homeward journey. The sum demanded for his release was £100,000, and all England had to pay it.

Any tenant was expected to pay for his lord's ransom, but these sums were not nearly enough. New taxes were invented and old ones revived; churches gave gold and silver vessels; a special tax of one-fourth was levied on all incomes; towns paid for their charters; even the sheep contributed! For certain monasteries owned large flocks and gave up all their year's profits on the wool.

The King was held captive for about seventeen months. His mother Queen Eleanor was active in collecting money, and although she assured her friend the Pope in a letter that she was worn to a skeleton, the old lady insisted on travelling to Cologne to greet Richard on his release. Hubert Walter conveyed the colossal ransom, and having delivered it safely, turned his attention to bringing the survivors of Richard's army back from Palestine. He also suppressed the revolt led by John. Hubert was made Archbishop of Canterbury as well as justiciar, and in Richard's latter years he practically ruled England.

The story is told of Richard singing in his prison and being heard by the minstrel who was looking for him. This, though a legend, has its grain of truth, because he is known to have written poetry in prison. He also had practical ability, being expert in the various catapult-like weapons that were used for hurling stones against castle walls. One weapon, the cross-bow, was introduced by him into France; and it was a bolt from one of them which proved fatal to himself.

Richard lost his life from a wound received when he was besieging the castle of Chaluz, to compel his tenant there to give up a treasure that had been found buried. Before he died, Richard sent for the man who had shot the bolt. The man arrived in a state of terror, but the dying King forgave him. He had also forgiven the treacherous behaviour of his brother John, who would now succeed him as king.

"I have lost the staff of my age, the light of my eyes," lamented Queen Eleanor, after Richard's death.

To England he must have meant little more than a name; and if the name of *Cœur de Lion* was surrounded with some awe and prestige, it was also perhaps associated in many minds with the not-so-romantic figure of the tax-collector.

KING RICHARD I
From his tomb at Fontevrault

2

King John, called Lackland, allowed the King of France to re-conquer Normandy and the other Plantagenet possessions in France.

He defied the Pope, who in reply put England under an Interdict that lasted over six years.

He provoked his tenants-in-chief in England, until they forced from him the great Charter (Magna Carta).

These three outstanding events in his reign are an indication of King John's character, and how his irresponsibility called out forceful action from others.

During the earlier years, when Normandy was slipping from his grasp, two people died who were trying to make John act as a responsible king: Queen Eleanor, aged eighty, and Archbishop Hubert Walter, whose death in 1205 left a vacancy at Canterbury. Here was the starting-point of John's struggle with the clergy.

Pope Innocent III, masterful and fearless, rejected both the man chosen by the Canterbury monks, and the man chosen by John, to succeed Hubert Walter; he appointed the man of his own choice, Stephen Langton.

John refused to accept Langton as Archbishop. Innocent then placed England under an Interdict and excommunicated John. The churches were shut; the property of the clergy was taken over by the King. Nearly all the bishops, deprived of their belongings and their work, and fearing for their lives, fled from the country. John was godless and did not care; the Church estates made him richer, which was a help now that there were no rents coming in from Normandy.

Langton, who had been at Rome when appointed, was a God-led man, and he did care. In great agony of mind he fulfilled his duties as Archbishop as far as he could from abroad, as it was impossible as yet for him to come to England.

In 1211 the Pope threatened that if John would not recall the bishops and restore what he had taken from them, he, Innocent, would release John's subjects from their duty to obey their king. John would be put off the throne and Innocent would charge Philip Augustus of France, John's enemy, with the duty of seeing that this was done.

John tried desperately with threats and bribes to gain support, or at least to gain time, but in vain. No one would take his side. In 1213 his resistance collapsed. He accepted Stephen Langton, welcomed him to England, fell at his feet weeping, promised to repay the clergy, promised homage to the Pope and laid his crown as a token at the feet of the Papal messenger. England became Innocent's fief. The Interdict was lifted; the church doors opened.

John had just managed to save his throne. He feasted and made merry. A poor hermit who had foretold that the King would be deposed within a year, was proved wrong and was cruelly dragged at a horse's tail through the town of Wareham and then hanged, by the King's orders.

3

Later in the same year a meeting was held at St Albans to assess the damage and reckon up how much money John must repay to the Church.

Along with barons and bishops, groups of five men could be seen at this gathering, each group from one of the royal manors. Four out of the five lived or worked on the land and the fifth was their reeve or foreman, who planned and oversaw each day's fieldwork. Probably these countrymen could not read or write, but they could tell what they knew and help to make a true total reckoning. There they sat with the lords and bishops in something like a national assembly, hearing—perhaps taking part in—serious discussion of national needs. The Charter of Liberties which Henry I had granted, may have been mentioned or read aloud. Hardly a person present but had suffered some unjust treatment from King John or his officers, and perhaps already the thought of another Charter was in some minds.

The King (who had not been present at St Albans) now disappeared from England for a while. He had hired troops to try to re-conquer Normandy. None of the barons felt bound to follow him overseas; his hopes were pinned on allies, who were enemies of the French and willing to attack Philip Augustus. But the campaign failed completely, and John "Softsword" (another of his nicknames) returned to England at the end of 1214, as much "Lackland" as before.

He found baronage and Church even more united and determined. They had met at Bury St Edmunds with their tenants fully armed, in a so-called pilgrimage which turned into a council of war. They swore that if John did not restore the laws and liberties they would make war on him until he gave them a sealed charter; and, swords in hand, they would answer for it that he kept his word.

John tried to stir up trouble between barons and clergy, but they stood firmly together. All he could do was to gain a little delay—a three months' truce. That gave time for the Charter to be thought out and because it was long and covered many points, it was called the "great" Charter (Magna Carta). Later generations came to appreciate it as "great", not in its size as a written document, but in the way it sketched great principles of political freedom.

When the three months' truce was up, the barons' army assembled in the Midlands and rode towards London, where the citizens gave them a noisy welcome. In the great Charter, London had a paragraph to itself.

John's courtiers and servants melted away, only seven knights being left to attend on him. Under the Archbishop's guidance the whole sixty-three paragraphs had been written out, and on June 15th, 1215, the King received the leaders at Runnymede and put his seal to the great sheet of parchment.

Magna Carta began: "John . . . to the archbishops, bishops, abbots, earls, barons, justiciars, foresters, sheriffs, reeves, servants, and all bailiffs and faithful men, greeting. Know that . . . by the counsel of Stephen Archbishop of Canterbury [and twenty-seven others named] I have granted and confirmed that the English Church shall be free . . ."

Although it dealt in detail with practical matters like property and payments that the King and others were entitled to have, the great Charter also made a few general statements, which were used in later times to protect the liberty of subjects and limit the power of kings. One of these is: "To none will we sell, to none will we delay or deny right and justice."

Thus did the far-seeing Archbishop act responsibly for the England that he knew and loved.

As they knew that John would only fulfil as much of the Charter as suited himself, the barons had chosen twenty-five men from among themselves to make sure that it was kept in full. They were right. Within a year, his attempts to break the promises to which he had put his seal had thrown the country into confusion, and the French King's son had been invited to come over and take his throne. But before anything decisive happened John died.

He showed signs of remorse for his sins at the very last, and carefully provided for his two sons—aged nine and eight—whom he loved: and this last, pathetic shred of fatherly responsibility is one, perhaps the only, pleasant glimpse to be had of John Lackland.

CHAPTER SIX

Henry III: Edward I: Edward II

I

Four copies of the Magna Carta still exist. We do not know which of them was actually handled at Runnymede, but anybody who wishes to see one need only go to the British Museum in London and ask. Two are there, and the others are at Salisbury and Lincoln.

One place that visitors to London must see sooner or later, is Westminster Abbey. Try to imagine the Abbey without the twin towers in the west, Henry VII's chapel in the east, and the monuments inside, all of which were added later, and what is left? A building of stately simplicity, whose lines rise high and meet in the curves of a gracefully vaulted roof.

Here is the monument and the life-work of Henry III, son of King John, the elder of the two boys John thought about on his death-bed.

Of course, Edward the Confessor built the first Abbey, but Henry III built another on the same site. Henry III lived in a time when there was immense activity in building churches and cathedrals, especially in France. He grew up under the guardianship of two Regents and Archbishop Langton, and became a devoted son of the Church. Later he had many ties with France. His wife, and the French king's wife, were sisters. The two kings, Louis IX (Saint Louis) of France and Henry III of England had much in common and there could well have been a friendly rivalry between them as there was between certain French cities, as to who should build the finest cathedrals.

Henry had seen Beauvais, Amiens and Reims which must have inspired him. Louis was having St Denys built as the burying-place of kings. Henry may have thought that the Westminster Abbey he had known from his boyhood looked out-of-date. At any rate he had it all pulled down, and in its place rose these clusters of slender columns supporting the lofty roof, with the outer walls flanked by flying buttresses, in the style called Early English.

The new Abbey, brilliantly decorated in colours within, had quite different proportions from the old, although it was still in the form of a cross. But the tomb of King Edward lay untouched at the heart of it;

34

and towards the end of the twenty-five years which the Abbey took to build, Henry had a new shrine made. The body of Edward the Confessor (he was now called Saint Edward) was transferred to the shrine, which can still be seen there, and on the wall above are sculptured panels with scenes from St Edward's life. At the ceremony a ring was removed from the dead king's finger, and the sapphire in the ring is thought to be the same as the large one now in the State Crown; if so, it is England's oldest Crown Jewel.

Henry reigned fifty-six years and had this great interest at the centre of his life, but as a king he was not very successful. He spent and gave away too much money, especially to the Provençals who came as attendants to his Queen, Eleanor of Provence. He let the Pope appoint Italian priests to English towns and villages who either did not understand the people or remained abroad, drawing their pay though themselves absent.

Rebellion by the barons—it sounds a familiar story—once more broke out. The barons' leader, Simon de Montfort, was an able soldier. He defeated the King and captured his eldest son, Prince Edward. For just over a year, Edward was in captivity, Henry was politely ignored and Simon, who had a high reputation as one who "loved right and hated wrong", ruled the land.

One of Simon's memorable actions was to call a meeting of the King's tenants-in-chief and to summon along with them two representatives of each shire, city and town. For the first time townspeople had spokesmen in a central national assembly, and to this gathering can be traced the beginnings of Parliament as we know it.

After twelve months in prison, Prince Edward escaped, defeated and killed Simon de Montfort, and restored his father to full authority.

Henry's last years were uneventful. They gave Edward the chance to ponder over what he had seen and profit by it when his own time came. He loved his father, but saw his mistakes; he hated Simon, but realised his wisdom.

Edward gave his father a splendid tomb at Westminster and had it suitably placed, close to that of St Edward.

2

Henry III had lived in a cathedral-making age; Edward I lived in a law-making age. Several other countries then were ruled by famous law-givers and Roman law was being studied at the universities.

KING HENRY III
From his effigy
in Westminster Abbey

KING EDWARD II
From his effigy
in Gloucester Cathedral

36

Edward as a boy lived mainly at Windsor. His tutor, Robert Burnell, was learned in the law, and became Chancellor when Edward was King. Much had been written about "the law", and Edward knew that kings are expected to live according to, and not above, the law.

It may be asked what, then, was "the law" of England and what did these writers mean. Edward disliked anything vague or confused. He had a clear brain and did not shrink from hard mental toil. Some of the law was already written, and already ancient; some of it was being made from day to day as cases were argued and judges gave judgment. He, too, as king, could consult his Great Council and issue Statutes that would bring punishment to those who disobeyed them.

Edward mastered the legal codes or lists drawn up by earlier kings from about A.D. 600 onwards. His first Statute, in which he said the law was to be the same for rich and poor alike, had fifty-one clauses and is almost a code in itself.

There followed other Statutes that concerned land-holding. They saved disputes for overlords and tenants would now know exactly what they owed, as well as what was owed to them.

Another of the old ideas that is not out-of-date, though now it takes different forms, is that ordinary folk can and should keep order; they should protect each other, and each other's houses, purses and property. Here he went right back to the Anglo-Saxons; he re-enacted the rule of "watch and ward". In walled towns, he wrote, sixteen men were to keep awake at the gates from sunset to sunrise, through the summer months; at smaller places in the country, six men, or four. They were called the watch. (He did not mention winter-time; it looks as if even would-be criminals preferred not to roam about then in the cold and darkness.)

There was as yet no uniformed police force, so the watch had to arrest suspicious characters, and if the evil-doer ran away, as of course he would, the "hue and cry" was raised. Anybody hearing it, day or night, had to join in the chase, from town to town and district to district. The man, if caught, was handed over to the sheriff. Edward ordered that along the roads each side, a strip 200 feet wide should be cleared of bushes and undergrowth, so as to make it difficult for the felon, or law-breaker, to hide, and then "return to do evil".

Edward tried to apply his ideas to Wales and Scotland, whose ancient laws were based not on land-holding but on clan customs. And although he forced the Welsh to divide their land into shires like those of England they did it unwillingly, and he failed altogether to bring Scotland into the framework he had planned, with himself as royal overlord.

What has just been said about Scotland is a rough summing-up of a long story. At one time Edward did almost succeed there, nearly every baron north of the Border having paid him homage. Many districts, too, were used to the feudal way of land-holding; that in itself was not a grievance, but meantime blood had been shed, English soldiers occupied Scotland as enemy country and by the close of Edward's reign Scotsmen of all classes were passionately determined to serve their own king, Robert Bruce, and be a nation under him—not a fief under Edward Plantagenet.

3

As the years went on, Edward became more and more involved in costly undertakings, chiefly these wars in Wales and Scotland and other wars in France. Even without fighting, he had to provide supplies for the garrisons in Scottish castles and to build a large number in Wales. He needed money so constantly that his usual income never seemed to bring in enough.

Edward had long known and agreed with the saying, "What touches all, should be approved by all." Taxes, or rather the tax-collector, "touched" all, in their pockets. Therefore he had to consult his chief tax-payers, the tenants-in-chief, ever more frequently, and by this time the plan of men coming to represent their communities—whether country or town—was not new. (See pp. 32 and 35.)

At Westminster Hall, in 1295, Edward met with his Council and with knights, townsmen and clergy—two from each shire, town and diocese. They discussed the King's request for a tax and agreed that it should be paid. The discussion was called a *parlementum*, i.e. a talking; and the same word was used later on for the people who talked. Edward held altogether about twenty-five "talkings" at different times, though not all of them included men from the shires.

A Statute today means a law when it is complete; whether it has to do with money or not, it has been approved by a majority in Parliament and has received the Sovereign's assent. The final words are *"Le Roy* [or *la Reine*] *le veult"*—"The King [Queen] wills it". These words remind us vividly of Edward I who thought, spoke and wrote in that kind of French.

When Edward died, he was a long way from Westminster; he was near Carlisle, close to the Scottish Border. He had started out in full military array to pursue King Robert whom he regarded as a felon, a traitor, a skulking rebel, but whom the Scots respected as their brave and beloved sovereign. Death stopped Edward from striking any more blows in that direction.

On his tomb, which was a severely plain one of grey marble, were inscribed the words *Pactum serva*, Keep troth, because Edward kept his word and expected others to do the same; and also *Scotorum malleus*, the Hammer of the Scots.

4

Edward II, son of Edward I, was born at Carnarvon Castle and is said to have been shown as an infant to the Welsh chiefs as their Prince. This is only a story, and in fact he was seventeen when he received the title of Prince of Wales, which since then has always been granted to the sovereign's eldest son.

Edward grew up a spoilt and handsome dandy of a prince; he wanted to be entertained and amused, or to gamble, all the time. As king he proved himself unfit to rule, having neither vigorous brain-power, nor manly virtues, nor trustworthy friends. He tried however to carry out his father's aim of subduing Scotland, and in 1314 after a year of preparation he took an army of about 20,000 men to relieve the English garrison which was shut up in Stirling; but at Bannockburn 7,000 Scots led by King Robert defeated him, and he fled from the battlefield.

From then onwards, Edward's affairs went from bad to worse. Finally, the same threat which had hung over his great-grandfather, King John, that of being deposed, was carried out. The Pope had nothing to do with it this time; the English did it themselves. One knight, speaking for the whole Parliament—and hence the whole country—renounced his homage and said he was no longer the King's man; the steward of the royal household broke his wand of office, betokening that Edward had ceased to reign. The King's son, another Edward, then aged fourteen, had already been brought into Westminster Hall and welcomed by shouts from the people; he was now acknowledged as the reigning king.

Eight months after his deposition, Edward II was murdered in his prison at Berkeley Castle, it is not known for certain by whom.

KING EDWARD III
From his effigy in Westminster Abbey

PLATE I

RICHARD II

PLATE II   HENRY IV

PLATE III   HENRY V

PLATE IV   HENRY VI

CHAPTER SEVEN

Edward III: Richard II

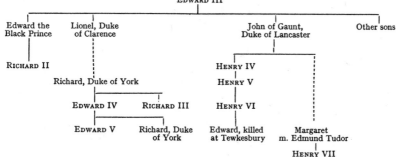

I

Edward III was a pleasure-lover rather than a hard-working lawyer like his grandfather. But he had staying-power, courage and the qualities that win battles.

To him, war may have looked like a game. It was like life-sized chess: you could take a castle here (and use all its provisions) and un-horse a knight there (and get his ransom). Best of all was the feat of capturing a king. Twice Edward had this satisfaction; the kings of Scotland (1346) and of France (1356) were both seen riding as captives through the streets of London.

One day in hand-to-hand combat with a French knight, Sir Eustace de Ribeaumont, Edward was twice brought to his knees; but he re-covered and captured Eustace. All the French prisoners dined in the English King's pavilion that evening, and he, wearing a coronet of pearls, afterwards moved about chatting with his "guests". He smilingly congratulated Eustace on being the best combatant of the day, and placing on the Frenchman's head the pearl coronet, let him go free without paying any ransom. Much admiration was expressed by those who saw the incident.

Edward was indeed a polished example of the code of knighthood, though chivalry no longer meant what it once did. In its earlier days, before being knighted the youthful squire used to spend a night in prayer in the House of God, and then after a bath, and clothing himself in a white tunic—white for purity—he put on outer garments of red—symbol of blood and sacrifice—and black, to show that he was mortal. He vowed to protect the weak and helpless and to fight for the right; and to those noble causes his sword was dedicated.

By men such as this the First Crusade had been won. Two and a half centuries later when Edward III reigned, chivalry had come to mean little else than tournaments, mock warfare, feasting and dancing and much attention to the ladies. Edward was enthusiastically chivalrous, and after having Windsor Castle enlarged and re-built he made it the scene of fantastic revels and gorgeous tournaments, besides founding there the Order of the Garter.

However, Edward's warfare was by no means all "mock". He began by terminating the long war with Scotland in 1328. It broke out again three years later. The Scots and French were in close alliance. Philip VI of France, in order to help his allies and distract the English, invaded Guienne, the only part of France (with one small exception) which remained to Edward out of the great Plantagenet inheritance. Guienne lies south of Bordeaux and astride the river Garonne. It was and is famous for its wines, and carried on a busy trade with England.

Edward went to war not only for the sake of Guienne, but also because he claimed to be himself the rightful King of France. He could do so because his mother (Isabella) was the daughter of a French king, Philip IV. His own Queen, Philippa, was not French, she came from Flanders; but her countrymen favoured Edward's claim and were his willing allies, because they were interested in the cloth trade and saw England as a better trade partner than France.

Even a brief list of Edward's early successful strokes is impressive. The English won a naval battle (Sluys) and two land battles (Crecy, Neville's Cross) besides capturing Calais, the doorstep into northern France. Crecy proved that English archers could shoot far and aim straight; Neville's Cross stopped a Scottish back-stab from the north, and yielded a royal prisoner. Masses of loot from France poured into English households—dresses, jewels, linen, even saucepans from French kitchens.

Yet Edward never reached Paris, and he never wore the French crown.

2

The peak of Edward's success was the Treaty of Bretigny (1360) which gave him most of the former Duchy of Aquitaine and a ransom of three million gold crowns for his captive, King John the Good (taken with his eldest son at the battle of Poitiers). The money meant at least as much to Edward as the "glory", because he was too extravagant ever to be able to pay his debts. Already two wealthy banking-houses in Florence had gone bankrupt because of the enormous loans which they had made him and which he had never repaid.

The Parliament on which Edward or his chamberlain had to rely for funds when all his normal income was spent had changed in several ways since the time of Edward I. The House of Lords and the House of Commons now sat separately. The Commons expected to be consulted about public affairs, and not merely asked to consent to such-and-such a tax. They used to bring forward petitions. "Let the King have pity on the hardships which the Commons suffer," they would say—Commons, of course, meaning the communities, town or county, for which these men spoke. So we hear of tax-collectors cheating, small traders being ruined, coiners issuing counterfeit coins ("let the issuers of false money be hanged," the Commons prayed the King), sturdy beggars refusing to work—and many another grievance. Most of the petitions would not have been needed if Edward's officials had been loyal, honest and diligent.

Fifty to sixty such petitions might come up in each session, each written on a large sheet called a Bill. Edward usually granted them, but did not always follow up his promises with acts. Still the members persisted, and some important Statutes began in this way. By now they expected that a Parliament would be summoned every year.

At the middle of the century, 1349–50–51, there was a gap for three whole years when neither Lords nor Commons met; when church-building stopped, trade dwindled, crops were not reaped, the law-courts shut and every kind of public business came to a standstill.

England in common with many other countries, was stricken by plague, the terrible Black Death. This was only the first of three visits of the plague to England in Edward's reign. The others were less deadly, but the third one occurred in a gloomy year, 1369. The Anglo-French war had started again and was going badly, and the court was mourning the death of Queen Philippa, who had been much loved.

3

Edward and Philippa had a large family. The eldest son, Edward the Black Prince, so-called because of his black armour, was governor of Gascony. He had married a Kentish widow named Joan Holland, and their son Richard, born at Bordeaux, was two when his grandmother Queen Philippa died. On the death of the Black Prince in 1376 this little lad became heir to the throne.

King Edward failed pitiably in body and mind during his last years. One of the late queen's waiting-women gained such power over him that she did what she liked, and gradually all posts that fell vacant were filled with her disreputable friends. She was not resisted by the King's next son, the Duke of Lancaster (known as John of Gaunt), who took charge during his father's illness. The woman, Alice Perrers, had a finger in every pie; she interfered in lawsuits and actually sat along with the judges on the bench to hear cases. She also wore Queen Philippa's jewels which she said she (Perrers) had been given by the King.

The Parliament of 1376 is remembered as the Good Parliament. In it were earnest men who realised that those evil influences at Court were bringing the country to ruin. They had 140 petitions ready to present. For the first time a Speaker or chairman was appointed by the House of Commons. He was Sir Peter de la Mare from Herefordshire.

Under his leadership the scandals were ruthlessly exposed and two ringleaders, the King's financial agent, Lyons, and his chamberlain, Latimer, were impeached, i.e. accused, and found guilty of colossal frauds. They were sent to the Tower and their goods were confiscated. Perrers had to leave the court.

This wind of clean air blowing through the corridors of Westminster was most unwelcome to John of Gaunt. He dismissed the Parliament and summoned another one, making sure that only his own supporters would be sent to it. Such a process is called "packing" a Parliament and flatly disobeys a Statute of Edward I, who had written that no great man or other person should, by malice or menace, disturb the holding of a free election. Gaunt then released the fraudulent financiers and allowed the ex-waiting-woman back to her old quarters; meanwhile, de la Mare was imprisoned.

King Edward's dim brain could not take in these happenings. He knew nothing about his people's petitions. When it was evident that his death was near, Alice Perrers took all the rings off his fingers and stealthily departed. (It may be only by chance, but the poet Langland, who wrote in this period, portrays the flaunting, scarlet-clad "Lady Meed", symbol of greed and materialism, with her ten fingers covered with rings.)

During the next few hours the old man was deserted by everyone except a kindly priest, who held a cross before his eyes, and heard him murmur "Jesus have mercy" just before he died.

4

The Crown was now to be worn by ten-year-old Richard. He inherited an England full of discontent, a court full of strife, a Treasury full of debts and a war that his country was losing.

One of his first acts was to let the Speaker de la Mare out of prison. John of Gaunt was now to have much less influence; the King's mother had the chief share in governing. Richard had been adored by his parents and was accustomed to getting his own way. He was an intelligent, spirited boy and meant to be a king who really reigned, not just a figurehead.

His behaviour at the time of the Peasants' Revolt when he was fourteen showed him to be brave and resourceful; and his marriage the following year to Anne of Bohemia was a happy one, only they had no children. Their court began to be a centre where the arts flourished. Westminster Hall was largely rebuilt under Richard's directions and roofed over with the carved oaks beams that are still to be seen. Richard himself could sing, play and act with a high level of talent. (One aid to civilised living, said to be introduced by him, was the handkerchief.) Some of his doublets were embroidered with gems; kings before him had worn jewelled *cloaks*, which were fine for dazzling the crowd when one rode in State, but Richard and Anne sparkled when they were at home as well. They enjoyed gathering like-minded, luxury-loving friends around them; money flowed like water and nobody worried about debts.

Richard, however, disliked all his uncles and could not get on with his senior Councillors. John of Gaunt had no love for his nephew and was suspected of aiming at the monarchy himself; but he did not oppose Richard violently, and sought an outlet for his ambitions away from England. The noble words written for his death-bed scene by Shakespeare may not portray the real John of Gaunt.

Apart from the Peasants' Revolt there were two main crises in Richard's reign before its dramatic ending. In the first of these, 1386–

87, his uncle Gloucester and four other lords accused a group of Richard's friends of treason. He refused to dismiss his friends, but was overcome by force and compelled to do so, one of his closest companions (the Earl of Oxford) being killed.

Richard kept his craving for revenge under control for ten years. During that time his wife died, and his grief was so wild that he ordered a palace where she had lived to be destroyed. Indeed it has been suggested that Anne's death so deeply wounded Richard that thereafter he was not fully sane.

The second crisis was reached in 1397, when Richard suddenly moved against the same five lords. Three were imprisoned or executed. The other two were pardoned, but later, when they quarrelled at a tournament, Richard banished them both from England, one for life and the other for ten years. The latter lord was Richard's cousin Henry of Bolingbroke, the son of John of Gaunt (who died early in 1399) and now head of the powerful family of Lancaster.

Richard next packed a Parliament, which appointed a Committee to deal with petitions, voted the King enough money to last his lifetime, and then dissolved itself. Richard hated Parliaments, especially after the "Merciless" one in 1387 had supported the five lords and attacked his own friends, and quite obviously now he intended never to call another one.

Bolingbroke in exile realised something of the alarm felt in England at Richard's self-will and tyranny. As Richard, contrary to his promise, had seized the Lancaster property, Bolingbroke landed in Yorkshire and gathered forces to bring him to account. Within a few weeks Richard was his prisoner. In presence of a hastily summoned (but freely elected) Parliament, Richard was compelled to yield the crown to his cousin, who was hailed as King Henry the Fourth.

From then onwards Richard was kept a prisoner in Pontefract Castle and within a year, by the end of 1400, he was dead—either killed by his gaoler or starved to death by his own will.

Thus tragically perished the last Plantagenet king. So too ended the fourteenth century, an age of luxury and cruelty—to quote Bishop Stubbs: "in which the gloss of superficial refinement fails to hide the reality of heartless selfishness and moral degradation."

CHAPTER EIGHT

Henry IV: Henry V: Henry VI

I

Before 1399, Henry of Bolingbroke seems to have led a care-free life. He had married Mary de Bohun, a wealthy heiress; they had four sons, he was respected at home, and although an opponent of Richard's headstrong actions he was himself moderate. He was zealous for the Church and twice had gone on a Crusade. Henry's eastern journeys may account for the unusual costume and head-dress in the portrait (p. 42).

In 1390, with a company of three hundred he sailed from Boston in Lincolnshire to Danzig, to join in a Crusade with the Order of Teutonic Knights against the heathen Lithuanians. The latter had recently begun to turn to Christianity, but the Teutonic Knights were still on the war-path. Henry and his Lincolnshire men helped to capture the Lithuanian capital. He gave gifts to many churches in Poland, ransomed two Englishmen imprisoned by the Poles and returned home within a year.

In 1392 he went to Danzig again, but while there decided to visit the Holy Sepulchre at Jerusalem. His journey turned into more of a sight-seeing tour than a Crusade. He visited Prague and Vienna, and then rode southwards through mountain passes to reach Venice, where the Doge gave him a fully equipped galley; he was rowed in it down the Adriatic Sea to the isle of Rhodes, and thence to Jaffa, and so made his way to the Holy City.

After a short stay there he returned via Cyprus to Venice, and no doubt recounted to the Doge what he had seen; he had taken every chance to visit ancient sites. Familiar with Latin, observant, witty, with a good memory, Henry kept to his life's end the power of "saying sharp things".

Then overland, by Milan and Pavia, through the Alps again, he headed north for England, but lingered a while in Paris. It was in the hot summer of this same year that the French king, Charles VI, suddenly went mad. Quarrels as to who should hold the reins of government began around him, leading to a split between the Burgundian and Armagnac parties, and to civil war.

With all this Henry of Bolingbroke was not concerned. He came home, his tour having taken eleven months, which considering the ground covered and the methods of travel in those days was a remarkably short time.

He evidently liked Paris, because in 1399 when Richard II sentenced him to banishment, he chose to go back there. He was given the use of a nobleman's mansion, and it was here that he made his life's most weighty decision—to make a bid for the English throne.

It is not easy to tell whether Bolingbroke was "ambitious" in doing so, or whether he obeyed his conscience. He certainly had support throughout from the Church's leaders. When Richard was deposed in Westminster Hall, the Archbishops of Canterbury and York each took the new king by a hand and led him to the vacant throne, where after a few moments kneeling in prayer he took his seat.

For Henry's coronation the golden eagle flask which still holds the sacred oil was made and used for the first time. He also founded a new Order, the knights of which had the honour of conducting the sovereign (who bathed in the City of London before being crowned) to Westminster Abbey, and so were named Knights of the Bath.

There seems no reason to think Henry was not genuine in wanting to to get rid of corrupt and tyrannical practices.

2

Always when a change of dynasty comes about, with or without bloodshed, the new monarch has to be wary. If not, he will likely be turned out again and may lose his life, because supporters of the former régime are sure to be plotting to reverse what has happened and put their own man back again; or if that cannot be, to do it for his son or near relation.

This need to be watchful gives a clue to Henry's attitudes and actions as king. Several risings of Richard's supporters, even after Richard was known to be dead, had to be dealt with. Henry put them down drastically and promptly. Leaders of the first one were beheaded without trial. Yet Henry seemed not too sure of his friends, and afraid of giving offence. He never treated the House of Commons high-handedly as Richard had done. All three Lancastrian kings were forced by shortage of money to rule through Parliament.

Henry was afraid, too, of new ideas that were being discussed among Churchmen. The followers of an Oxford theologian, John Wyclif, had been bold to attack Papal demands and clerical corruption. These protesting voices, whether of laymen or the clergy themselves, were growing louder, and Parliament with Henry's approval decided that they should be silenced by a Statute ordering heretics to be burned.

In his later years Henry's conscience may have been uneasy. It was noticed that he liked arguing to justify himself, as if he needed to be reassured about what he had done. Was it right to have stopped these men expressing their opinions? Had he, Henry, been right when he seized the throne from his cousin Richard? Or was he a usurper?

Henry's thoughts cannot be followed now; what is certain is that he suffered much pain and ill-health latterly, with fainting fits, and a disease of the heart, and a skin trouble that was thought to be leprosy. It may well have been a relief to this well-meaning but care-worn king when death released him at the age of forty-six.

3

Henry V was not troubled, like his father, with rebellions. He succeeded smoothly to the throne, the dynasty of Lancaster being now recognised and no other claimant in sight than himself, his father's eldest son. His reign, though short, is memorable for the renewal of the war with France, begun long before by Edward III.

Henry took advantage of the confusion in France and the rivalries round the French throne, due to the madness of Charles VI. He invaded northern France, won the battle of Agincourt against heavy odds, and thrust deep into the Seine valley. His campaign continued successfully until he was able to gain a treaty that Edward III would have envied.

The Treaty of Troyes (1420) confirmed that Henry should keep all the land he had already conquered; it pledged him the support of one of the great rival parties—the Burgundians; it gave him the hand of the French king's daughter Catherine in marriage, with the promise that he should succeed to the throne.

One son, Henry, was born of this marriage. When the infant prince was eight months old, his father died. Two months later his grandfather, the King of France, also died. Thus the baby Henry became king of both countries.

4

The Duke of Bedford, uncle of Henry VI, was his Regent. Bedford was pro-Burgundian and anti-Armagnac. Together the English and the Burgundians controlled Paris, where at the age of nine Henry was solemnly crowned.

But Paris is not the whole of France. Elsewhere the Armagnacs stood up for the son of Charles VI, their Dauphin. At the time of Henry's crowning the tide had begun to turn. The Dauphin had been crowned in Reims. A new spirit of courage, determination, loyalty and unity had been born in the French people.

The next years saw the triumphing of that spirit, and along with it the discouragement, defeat and departure of the English soldiers.

Henry was brought up almost entirely in England. His mother, the widowed Catherine, married again. Her second husband was a Welsh landowner named Owen Tudor and they had two boys, Henry's half-brothers Jasper and Edmund.

His first teacher, who died when the boy was nine, was a monk. When Henry was twelve he stayed for three months at the Abbey of Bury St Edmunds. The place and the life there fascinated him; the monks made him a "Confrater", counting him as one of themselves. In all the ups and downs of his stormy life Henry found comfort in the company of religious men; and much later on, a wandering fugitive, he put on a monk's habit and lived for a while in a monastery in Yorkshire.

At the age of about seventeen he planned to found a college for prayer and good works, a place where poor boys should have free schooling. In this way Eton began, and connected with it was Henry's College at Cambridge, called "King's". At both of them the tall, slender young King stooped to lay the chapel foundation-stones with his own hands.

Henry was gentle and generous. He was surrounded by courtiers and nobles who were just the opposite. The country badly needed men of honour who would see that order was kept and laws were obeyed; its affairs had got out of hand and in the meantime the English conquests in France were slipping away.

If Henry lacked firmness, his wife did not, she was as hard as steel. The marriage between Margaret of Anjou and Henry VI was arranged as part of a peace plan during the last stages of the Hundred Years' War. In 1453 that war officially ended, and of all England's former possessions in France only Calais was left.

In the same year Queen Margaret gave birth to a boy. But when this baby was shown to the King, he only stared vacantly, not seeing the

ETON COLLEGE CHAPEL

child. His reason, memory and power of speech were all gone. For over a year this mental illness made him totally unfit.

Margaret would have acted for him as Regent, but two strong-willed men stood in her way, one of them related to the King, the other the head of the House of York. Quarrels about the Regency exploded and did not cease when Henry became normal again. They turned into a struggle for the crown itself, and came to be called Wars of the Roses, because the family badge of the House of Lancaster was a red rose and that of York a white one.

Several times peace could have been made, but Margaret refused to be reconciled with the Yorkists. She would not accept defeat either. When her forces were beaten in battle she retreated northwards and sought help in Scotland. In Wales, too (the country of Henry's half-brothers, the Tudors), sympathy was strong with the Lancastrians. In Ireland and France as well, Margaret laboured to raise men and money for her husband's cause.

55

The Yorkists had the upper hand as long as they could count on the most powerful noble of all, the Earl of Warwick, who had estates in twenty shires. With his help the Yorkist leader was made king, as Edward IV, while poor Henry after long wandering and many adventures was captured and put in the Tower of London.

However, when Warwick changed sides, the Lancastrian fortunes revived, and for a brief while Henry was restored to the throne with Warwick as his "Lieutenant" of the Kingdom. The captive King was taken from his wretched cell, given clean clothes and re-installed in Westminster Palace. But he was incapable of governing: one observer likened him to a sack of wool, while another said he was mute like a crowned calf. Margaret meantime, with their young son Edward, was busy in France, while Edward of York, their enemy, was trying to get recruits in Flanders.

Henry's second "reign" only lasted six months. The Yorkists came over from Flanders. Henry, who longed for peace, said to Edward, "Cousin, you are welcome." But he could not prevent Warwick and Edward—once friends and allies, and now bitter foes—from fighting to the death. In the Battle of Barnet, fought in a fog, Warwick fell headlong to the ground in his heavy armour, could not rise again and was killed.

About the same time Margaret, with her son and all the French troops she had collected, landed in the south-west, and made for the midlands; but the Lancastrians were scattered, and young Edward was killed, in the "bloody meadow" at Tewkesbury.

The White Rose had won, the Red Rose was doomed. Henry was once more led to the Tower and locked up. There, the very same night that Edward of York (Edward IV) re-entered London victoriously, the innocent Henry, meek and forgiving to the last, was stabbed to death.

Who did this deed? History cannot answer with certainty, but many people at the time thought that if the dagger was not actually held, the orders were given by one man who was definitely in the Tower that night: Edward of York's younger brother, Richard Duke of Gloucester.

CHAPTER NINE

Edward IV: Edward V: Richard III

I

After the deaths of her son and her husband, Queen Margaret's force was all spent. She saw no more hope for the Lancastrian side and only wished to die herself. She spent her last years in Anjou, depending on the goodwill of her cousin the King of France, who made her a small allowance, and there she died in poverty and vexation of spirit.

Edward IV was firmly established and was the father of a family; his wife was an English lady, Elizabeth Woodville. For some years there was no trouble about the succession, as Edward had two little sons (Edward and Richard) as well as several daughters.

Yet when Margaret of Anjou left England for good, the Red Rose party were not left wholly leaderless. Their link with the Lancastrian House was another woman—another Margaret—an English girl directly descended from John of Gaunt. She was Lady Margaret Beaufort, who when barely fourteen had been married to Edmund Tudor, the younger half-brother of Henry VI.

Edmund died in a plague in the second year of his marriage, and before his son was born. This son, named Henry, was a delicate baby and the young mother had many anxious moments about him, but her brother-in-law Jasper looked kindly on her distress and sheltered them both in his castle of Pembroke, where the child Henry Tudor spent most of his early years.

When he was fourteen, in the year of the Barnet and Tewkesbury battles (1471), all the advisers around Lady Margaret were convinced that the boy's life would be in danger if he remained where he was, as he was clearly the nearest Lancastrian to the throne and the triumphant Yorkists would want to make an end of him. She was urged to send him to France, and with a heavy heart she decided to let him go, but to remain in England herself. Some day she hoped he would gain the throne, though at the moment it seemed impossible, and she could do more to help him on this side of the Channel.

Henry Tudor sailed away south from Tenby under the care of his

uncle Jasper. Storms drove them on to the coast of Brittany. The Duke here was a sympathiser, and Henry remained a long-staying guest at his court. Meanwhile his mother who had married again (a son of the Duke of Buckingham) watched events in England and showed to Edward IV and his Yorkist relations a correct and prudent attitude; warm friendship was hardly to be expected.

One taste she had in common with the reigning King was that both were interested in books and eager to take advantage of the new invention of printing. In 1477 William Caxton set up his press in Westminster and was visited by Edward IV who wanted to see how it worked. Lady Margaret possessed a number of books, both in French and English.

She had "a holding memory", we are told, and a ready wit, she was small in stature, dignified in movement; her many friends loved her gentle, affectionate ways and charming manners.

One of her husband's retainers named Reginald Bray became a reliable agent and messenger between the lady and her son. In 1482 Henry was told of the death of his stepfather, and of his mother's intention to marry a third time. Her new bridegroom, the Earl of Derby, had been an active Yorkist, but evidently she hoped to persuade him to forget the past and work for Henry's return in the future.

News came to Henry in 1483 (April) that King Edward was dead and that his thirteen-year-old son was his successor; following this the late King's brother the Duke of Gloucester had hurried down to London from Yorkshire to get himself proclaimed Protector of the Kingdom (May 4th); London was filled with his retainers and buzzing with rumours. The young King Edward V had been removed to the Tower, where his eleven-year-old brother Richard Duke of York had been sent to join him. The Queen, his mother, and her daughters had taken refuge with the monks at Westminster.

The next sensation was reported at the end of May: the Protector Gloucester had been proclaimed King, Richard III (May 26th). What had happened to Edward V and his brother was a mystery; it still is. Had they both died from natural causes, or been smuggled away; and if so, where to? Or was it true, as people were saying, that they had been murdered—smothered with pillows as they lay asleep; and if so, by whose orders?

What account of their disappearance Henry received in Brittany cannot be known; but without doubt the two boys vanished off the scene, the Queen their mother was ill with grief and their uncle Richard was King.

2

Henry would be able to form some picture of the opponent he had never seen—Richard, short and swarthy, walking always with one shoulder higher than the other. Perhaps too he realised something of the fear this crooked little man inspired, and the utter disgust and weariness felt by many, at the seemingly endless story of quarrels, plots, battles and executions in the struggle for power.

In the meantime Lady Margaret, surrounded by Yorkists, behaved discreetly; in King Richard's coronation procession she carried his Queen's train of crimson velvet edged with miniver, and herself wore crimson velvet and cloth of gold. (This Queen had been Anne Neville, and was Warwick's daughter.) But some among the old red-rose nobility were sickened with Richard's methods of winning a throne. The Duke of Buckingham (father of Lady Margaret's second husband, and made Lord High Constable by Richard) left the Court angrily when he heard the fate of the two boys in the Tower, and rode away towards his estates in Wales.

On the way there he was met by Lady Margaret and they discussed together a plan to bring Henry back into England and marry him to one of Edward IV's daughters. Buckingham realised that this match would be an alliance of Lancaster with York, and would be welcome to both factions; furthermore, if Henry could be king as well, England could become united as it had never been in living memory.

When Buckingham reached his home at Brecon he spoke of the plan to Bishop Morton, another Lancastrian diehard; together they sent for Reginald Bray. Through him, the idea was put to Henry, and Lady Margaret was asked to see whether the widowed queen, still at Westminster, would give her consent. The most suitable of the daughters for Henry was considered to be the eldest, Elizabeth, then aged eighteen. Queen Elizabeth could easily be approached, for she had not yet recovered from her illness, and was being frequently visited by a Welsh physician whom Lady Margaret knew. At the interview which he arranged, the consent of both mother and daughter was willingly given.

Now every man who was known to dislike King Richard, and there were not a few, could be enlisted in the plot. Armed men were secretly placed at suitable points from South Wales to London, and throughout the south-west, to be ready for Henry's return from Brittany.

But the rising that was hoped for was a failure. King Richard was already on the watch. All over the south from Kent to Devonshire the rebels were ready, but they could not join up with Buckingham's force from Wales. Storms and heavy autumn rains raised the Severn, carried away bridges and flooded fields. The river took ten days to go down. The same storms scattered Henry's fleet coming over from Brittany. Buckingham was seized by Richard's men, tried to escape in disguise, was recaptured and was beheaded without trial. Lady Margaret's life was spared, only her lands were confiscated; and Richard, scorning her because she was a woman, told her husband to keep her at home so that she could not send any more letters or messages.

If Richard thought his words were going to stop her, he did not know much about women, especially mothers.

Eighteen months later all was ready for a second attempt. Richard had tried to bribe the Bretons to give Henry up to him—but they would not—and to bully the Princess Elizabeth into refusing him—but she would not. In August 1485 Henry and his friends, Bishop Morton, Jasper Tudor, Reginald Bray and many others, collected their fleet and sailed in a week without mishap to Milford Haven. Owing to his mother's careful planning and unceasing work beforehand, all went well.

The rest of the story is well known. At the Battle of Bosworth Richard's forces were defeated; Richard, fighting furiously to the last, was killed; the crown that he had been wearing over his helmet rolled off, and after the battle was found in a hawthorn bush, and picked up by Reginald Bray.

PLATE V   EDWARD IV

PLATE VI   RICHARD III

Anno h o s te octobz imago henrick VII trauruz rege illustrullimū
ordinata p henriami zmik Lo rege m unicion

PLATE VII   HENRY VII   *Att. to Michiel Sitium*

PLATE VIII   HENRY VIII   *After Holbein*

CHAPTER TEN

Henry VII

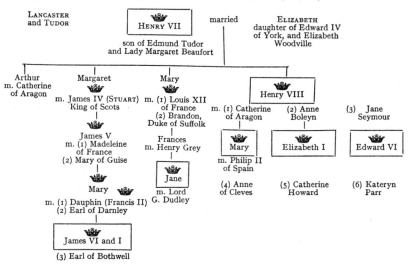

HENRY VII AND HIS DESCENDANTS

Reigning sovereigns, not consorts, marked with a crown. Names of sovereigns of England in ruled box.

I

Of all the English kings before him, Henry VII most resembled Henry IV. Both began new dynasties, and both had to tread with caution.

Henry VII found two "pretenders" claiming the throne. One was caught, but pardoned and given a job in the royal kitchen. The other went round neighbouring countries stirring up trouble and was so persistent that when caught he was executed. This was exceptional: Henry was not bloodthirsty but he could be ruthless when threatened.

He did not want to appear merely a conqueror, but to be the people's choice. Soon after Bosworth he called a Parliament, and by it was recognised as lawful sovereign. Then his marriage to Elizabeth of York pleased another whole section—the Yorkists—and turned out well.

Perhaps Henry's most sensible precaution, both for himself and England, was the Statute forbidding anyone to have retainers. The lords could have *servants*, as many as they liked, but must not deliver to them badged uniforms, nor weapons of war; there must be no more private armies.

Henry rewarded all who had helped to make him king. His uncle Jasper got a Dukedom, while Bishop Morton (now Cardinal) went to Canterbury. Bray was knighted and made Treasurer; he now turned his inventive mind to architecture and worked for some years on St George's Chapel at Windsor, where his initials can be seen. The Lady Chapel at Westminster Abbey was also begun in Henry's reign.

As for the King's mother, her lands were given back, naturally, and he gave her many more castles and manors. But she did not wish for thanks and honours. It was enough for her to see Henry, and it is recorded that at his coronation, "in all that grete tryumphe and glorye, she wepte mervaylously".

2

Henry VII was prudent, even sometimes thought stingy, in finance, but he left a full Treasury and prosperous country in the end.

These were times to be ready for new ventures and voyages to unknown lands. A vast continent new to Europeans was reached across the Atlantic, and trade with India was opened up. Henry was keen that England should share in oceanic enterprises, and with his goodwill two Genoese mariners (the Cabots) set sail from Bristol to be eventually the discoverers of Newfoundland.

As his family increased, the careful Henry thought about marriage-alliances for his children, with royal families abroad rather than noble ones at home.

Henry and Elizabeth had four children to plan for, besides three who died very young. The eldest son was christened Arthur. The choice of that name is interesting. In 1485 Caxton had published Sir Thomas Malory's collection of stories, *Morte Darthur*, about the legendary hero whose memory still lived in the valleys of Wales and in Brittany, scenes of Henry's boyhood. Perhaps Henry wanted Yorkist-sounding names like Edward and Richard to be forgotten, whereas "Arthur" was a kind of compliment to the Welsh.

The other royal children were named Margaret, Henry and Mary. Arthur was married when he was fifteen to Catherine, daughter of the King of Aragon. When she arrived, the young bride rode on a mule through London—every window on the route being crammed with spectators—clad in her Spanish finery and wearing "a littill hatte" made like a Cardinal's, tied on with gold cords under her chin. Lady Margaret gave a magnificent dinner party in her honour, each Spanish guest sitting next an English one.

The arrival of fourteen-year-old Margaret for her wedding to James IV, King of Scots, would be equally interesting to the citizens of Edinburgh; it took place at Holyrood in 1503.

Mary only married after her father's death. Then, aged seventeen, she became the bride of Louis XII, the elderly King of France and much-loved "father of his people". (He did not long survive his marriage and was said to have been danced into his grave by Mary's untiring energy, as she wore out her shoes by dancing all night.)

But those who rejoiced over the Spanish match in 1501, were mourning five months later, when Prince Arthur died.

The King, who lost his wife also, within a year, went on with his routine work, interviews, signatures, journeys or "progresses" round the country. At the time of the victory at Bosworth his eyes were described as "grey, shining and quick". In these latter years his sight was failing; it took him three days, for which he apologised, to finish writing a letter to his mother, and it proved to be his last one. He died in January 1509, and in June of the same year she followed him: both were buried in Westminster Abbey.

67

CHAPTER ELEVEN

Henry VIII

I

The personal history of Henry VIII is closely interwoven with that of his country.

He did as he chose and became practically a dictator, but England on the whole did not object. To start with Englishmen liked their jovial King Harry, who had a fine presence and was a splendid sportsman, dancer and musician. Even when he was middle-aged, fat and bad-tempered, few opposed him.

He lived in times of sweeping change when Christendom was dissolving into separate nations, and when large sections of people broke away from the Catholic Church to form new religious bodies.

As soon as Henry, aged eighteen, became King he married Catherine, the Spaniard, his brother Arthur's widow, thus carrying on the idea that England and Spain together could outmatch France. Yet friendship with France was symbolised a few years later by the marriage of Henry's sister Mary to the elderly French King. This grouping of the nations however did not last. It was part of the scheme devised by one of Henry's cleverest servants, Cardinal Thomas Wolsey, to raise England to a new proud eminence in Europe, and although Wolsey rose high in the King's esteem his plans were not well-founded.

Personal and national threads of history combined again when Henry grew tired of his wife Catherine. They had a daughter, Mary, but no son; and Henry fell in love with a court lady, Anne Boleyn. Personal matters, certainly, but they were taken into politics when Henry asked the Pope to declare the marriage with Catherine unlawful, so as to leave him free to marry Anne. The Pope refused, unwilling to offend Catherine's relations, especially her nephew who ruled the largest collection of States in Europe, the Holy Roman Empire, and having conquered Rome, practically held the Pope prisoner. Wolsey, who acted as Henry's agent, was blamed for the Pope's refusal. The full weight of the King's wrath fell on him. Deprived of all his posts and possessions, he died in disgrace.

Already men had defied the Pope because their conscience led them to do so. Henry now defied the Pope in order to obtain his own wish. He used his people's discontent with the Papal court and its demands for money; he used their complaints about bad character in monks or priests; and with a pliant Parliament he set to work to cut every tie that had bound the Church in England for hundreds of years to the Papacy. He, instead of the Pope, was to be the Church's Supreme Head (1534).

While these steps were being taken Henry secretly wedded Anne Boleyn. Thomas Cranmer, Archbishop of Canterbury, deemed their marriage valid and crowned Anne as queen.

After three years of married life, during which their daughter Elizabeth was born, Henry grew suspicious and accused Anne of various crimes; she was unable to defend herself and was executed.

Henry's conduct aroused dismay and disapproval in many at this point, but few dared to express their feelings. Two outstanding servants of Church and State, Bishop Fisher and Sir Thomas More, lost their lives because they would not swear to accept Henry as supreme over the Church.

So the break with Rome continued. Bishops were told to preach Royal Supremacy every Sunday, and have the Pope's name blotted out from every book. Finally the monasteries throughout the country were closed and the King took over their lands and money. Long before this, his extravagance had squandered the store of his father's wealth.

Henry next married Jane Seymour who gave him the son he so much wanted, but she did not long survive the birth of her child. After her death Thomas Cromwell, a very able lawyer who had helped Henry with drafting the anti-Papal laws and who had organised the dissolution of the monasteries, suggested for Henry another marriage-alliance, with Anne of Cleves. It was designed to link England with those princes of the Empire who had formed a Protestant League against the Pope. The King agreed and married Anne, but as she proved to be unacceptable to him personally, he sent her home again and in a rage with Thomas Cromwell, charged him with treason and sent him to the beheading-block.

2

Henry's two remaining marriages, unlike the earlier ones, had little to do with public affairs and were only of interest to court circles. Catherine Howard was young and attractive as Anne Boleyn had been; but like her, Catherine aroused Henry's suspicion, and was beheaded. His next bride, whose maiden name was Kateryn Parr, belonged to a north-country family and was already a widow. A capable, kind-hearted little woman, she looked after him when he was ailing, and was a good stepmother to Edward (Queen Jane's son) who passed his childhood in these extraordinary surroundings. She, the sixth of Henry's queens, outlived her husband.

Wolsey, More, Cromwell—three Thomases—all had collided with Henry's massive will-power and each met his own fate. The fourth Thomas, Archbishop Cranmer, was subservient and survived Henry's reign, though he perished for the Protestant cause in 1556. At every turn their story underlines how the break with Rome and the beginning of the Reformation came about through "the strong, intelligent, self-willed force of the King".

Yet Henry never meant to create a new Protestant Church, or alter what was taught about religion. The teaching inherited from the past through Rome was to go on.

3

A fifth Thomas came up against the will-power of Henry VIII. His story begins further back, in the reign of the first Plantagenet king.

In 1170, Henry II had permitted a Norman baron holding Welsh estates to go over and aid the King of Leinster, a rebel against Ireland's High King. The baron did so, was well rewarded, settled in Ireland and was followed by many other land-hungry adventurers. Henry II called himself Lord of Ireland, and after his time there were no more Irish High Kings.

The title "Lord of Ireland" was kept by the next English kings, though in fact it meant little. Each one appointed a Lord Deputy, who ruled for him in Dublin, but only controlled the city and a limited area outside.

Under Henry VIII, the Deputy belonged to one of those families descended from Norman adventurers, but by now fully rooted in Ireland: the Fitzgeralds. The head of this family, the Earl of Kildare, was summoned to London in 1533 and accused of treasonous plotting with the Irish. He was kept in the Tower and his son "Silken Thomas" (so-called from his liking for fine clothes) took his place as Deputy in Dublin. A report reached the son that the father had been beheaded. Silken Thomas at once rode to St Mary's Abbey in Dublin where the

Council of State was in session, flung the Sword of State on the table
and exclaimed, "I am none of Henry's Deputy, I am his foe!"

These words signalled the beginning of a rebellion. It was crushed
with the aid of troops that Henry sent over, and with what the Irish
called the "foreign grey gun", they themselves only having old-
fashioned weapons. The Fitzgeralds met the fate that might have been
expected. Thomas, his father and five uncles all were beheaded and
only one male member of the family (Thomas's young brother) was
lucky enough to escape.

Henry's next move was to have castles built in different parts of
Ireland, and the country was overawed by their English garrisons. The
Parliament in Dublin did not dare to do anything but follow what the
"Reformation" Parliament in England had been doing; similar Acts
were passed, Henry became Supreme Head of the Church, and the
monks were turned adrift. In 1541 Henry VIII, still ruling through a
Lord Deputy, took the title King of Ireland.

The last years of his reign saw no disorders there. It was an unreal
peace, the quietness of fear, a lull before many storms.

71

CHAPTER TWELVE

Edward VI: Jane Grey: Mary I

I

Edward VI succeeded according to his father's Will; at the time he was only nine. His first Protector (and uncle), the Duke of Somerset, held definitely Protestant views. In his opinion, Henry VIII had rightly spurned the Pope's rule, but had not gone far enough. Somerset had the images of saints removed from the churches and destroyed. A Prayer Book in English, mainly written by Cranmer, was published to replace the Latin service books.

Somerset planned that Edward should some day marry Mary, Scotland's child-queen; the boy-king was nine, she was five. But Somerset's method of asking was so rough that Mary's mother (who was French, and a Catholic) would not listen to his proposals and sent the little girl away to France to be brought up there; later to be married to the Dauphin of France.

Edward was not fond of his uncle, but did not give him trouble. He liked his tutors (Cheke and Cooke who were eminent scholars) and worked hard at Scripture, French, Latin and Greek, besides learning mathematics, geography and astronomy. About a dozen boys of noble families worked and played along with him. The one he liked best, Barnaby, was called his whipping-boy and was supposed to take his place if he had to be beaten, which did not happen often.

Most of his time Edward spent between the palaces of Whitehall and Greenwich, and in summer he would go out to Hampton Court, so he must have been familiar with the Thames and all its barges and ferries and rowing-boats. He was worried by the number of beggars and tramps to be seen in London, and gave a royal house there to be used as a centre providing work for unemployed men.

Although Edward showed little affection for Somerset, he was just as keen a Protestant as his uncle. The second Protector, who took over when Edward was fourteen, had still more extreme views, though no real religious convictions. This pushing courtier, Northumberland, had despised Somerset as inefficient, schemed to bring about his fall and

PLATE IX   EDWARD VI   *After Holbein*

PLATE X

LADY JANE GREY

took his place; he only took a strong Protestant line because he thought that would best serve his family interests.

Edward wrote a Journal* from the time he was ten and steadily kept it going, but the record breaks off just after he turned fifteen. Earlier that year he had measles followed by smallpox, which must have left him exhausted and weak.

In January 1553 Edward caught cold, after getting overheated playing tennis. (This was the indoor game, not *lawn* tennis; his father had been a keen player too in his time.) Edward could not throw off the cold and it developed into a cough and then into consumption.

Protector Northumberland persuaded the boy to make a Will, as everyone realised that his death might be near. By it, Edward cancelled his father's bequest of the Crown to his older half-sisters, Mary and Elizabeth. Instead, urged on by the Protector, he willed it to his Protestant cousin, the Lady Jane Grey. She was then sixteen and had just married Lord Guildford Dudley, Northumberland's son.

Northumberland is therefore seen grabbing the Crown, as it were, from the dying boy's fingers, for his daughter-in-law, and ensuring for himself the most influential position in the country as soon as Edward should cease to breathe. . . .

Edward died in the arms of a faithful attendant, on a summer's day, while the river flowed quietly past his window.

He was not yet sixteen, and had the makings of a fine king.

2

Mary, daughter of Henry VIII and Catherine of Aragon, and as true a Catholic as ever breathed, was set aside by her Protestant brother's Will, yet she won the Crown within a fortnight of his death—and remained queen till her own—because she took a quick, bold decision then, and also because it was clear that England wanted her.

Northumberland, to place Lady Jane successfully on the throne, would need to imprison Mary. Yet even before she knew of Edward's death, Mary felt strongly that she was in danger. She decided to leave the house where she usually lived; she rode away to join Catholic friends in Norfolk where she felt safe—a long ride of a hundred miles.

Her enemy thus could not lay hands on her, and meanwhile caused his daughter-in-law to be proclaimed queen. Nothing was further from Jane's wishes. She was a gentle, studious girl who loved her books and

* It is now in the British Museum.

her country home in Suffolk. With young Dudley she could have led a normal, happy life.

But she could not well refuse, and so for nine days she actually was Queen of England. Meanwhile Mary had herself proclaimed, and instantly won so much support that when Northumberland went to arrest her, his own troops turned against him. His opponents on the Council then disowned Jane and compelled him to submit to Mary.

Mary married Philip II of Spain, a country which without wavering held to Catholicism. There was no question whatever in Mary's mind what she must do. To the joy of many and the dismay of some, she and her Parliaments reversed all the laws that were anti-Catholic in the previous reigns; the Pope's supremacy was restored. (Only the monastery lands were left as they were, and not given back to the monks.)

But these actions called out strong opposition. Then the laws against heresy were revived in full force and spared neither leaders nor lay people among the Protestants. Two Protestant bishops were burned alive, and Cranmer, who had wavered and had stated that he was a Catholic, realised that he had done so out of fear, and bravely met the same death as his Protestant companions.

Other Protestants, up to the number of nearly three hundred, died in this way as well and their steadfast courage deeply impressed the mass of people who hitherto had not felt greatly stirred either way.

In spite of all her efforts, then, Mary could not feel that everything was just the same as before. The Reformation, whether one liked it or not, was a fact. She was disappointed also in the hope that she might have had a son who would inherit the Catholic faith of his parents and some day unite the crowns of England and Spain. She had no child, and the alliance of the two countries only involved England in Spain's quarrels.

War between France and Spain resulted in an enlargement of the French kingdom and the surrender of Calais to the French. For English pride this was a hard blow. Hence Queen Mary's life, which ended the same year as the loss of Calais, ended in gloom.

The Protestants who only remembered the blazing fires which had devoured the martyrs in Mary's reign, called her Bloody Mary; but in the long run history has been kinder to this unhappy woman, as one who had to endure much and was never anything but single-minded and sincere.

CHAPTER THIRTEEN

Elizabeth I

I

"Queen Bess was Harry's daughter." In this line Kipling expresses something of the affectionate loyalty of the English towards their great Queen, while suggesting that she inherited her father's kingly qualities.

She was tall and strong, she had his shining golden-red hair, she was highly educated, she excelled at dancing and music, and like Henry VIII she could quickly and realistically grasp any situation. Unlike him, she had learned to control her feelings and be patient; sometimes she appeared undecided when really she was only waiting for the right moment to act. Her decisions, or seeming lack of them, form the central core of her story.

She had only reigned three days when she chose an excellent Secretary, William Cecil, who remained her right-hand man till his death in 1598.

Obviously the first question demanding an answer was, whether to take a firm Protestant stand like Edward VI, or bring the Church back to what it had been in her father's time—with Catholic teaching yet no obedience to the Pope.

The Catholic Church had made a gigantic effort to purge out its faults and was now determined to win back heretics and conquer the world for Catholicism. The spearhead of this Counter-Reformation was the Jesuit Order, whose self-sacrificing and highly-trained members though based in Rome were ready to go to the ends of the earth.

Philip II fully shared these aims. He now ruled Spain, Portugal, the Netherlands (modern Holland and Belgium) and all the islands and colonies gained by his countrymen throughout the world.

France, which lost a strong king in 1559, was dominated for the next thirty years by the fanatical Catholic queen-mother Catherine. Many Frenchmen had turned Protestant, and during those years wave after wave of frightful civil wars (called Wars of Religion) shook the country.

The Holy Roman Empire, where the Protestant movement had

77

begun, was also divided in opinion; but there the formula that each Prince settled for his own State its form of religion, kept peace for the moment.

Elizabeth's decisions, then, were those of a woman who knew she was set in the midst of many and great dangers. She answered the Church question in a way that satisfied most of her subjects and though it did not—could not—please them all, has shaped the structure of the Church of England ever since. Bishops were to have authority under her, the Supreme Governor; and the Prayer Book was to be used. Catholics were not to be ill-treated, only fined for not attending church. Elizabeth was no fanatic.

She had many chances and offers of marriage, but never married, preferring not to commit herself to any permanent alliance, and yet to be able to use in diplomatic bargaining the *possibility* of her marriage.

She decided to help the Scottish Protestants in a crisis when they asked her to, but she could not prevent Mary, their Catholic queen who returned from France soon after, from drawing to herself as if with a magnet the loyal hopes of every Catholic in Britain.

Elizabeth also helped the Dutch Protestants when they rebelled against Philip of Spain. To both Scots and Dutch she only sent aid reluctantly, she disliked supporting *any* rebels against their rulers and she grudged spending money; still, in her judgment these were moments when it had to be done.

When Mary, Queen of Scots, was forced to abdicate, and fled into England, Elizabeth took no decisive action. Almost anything she might have chosen to do, would have been a dangerous mistake. She kept Mary as her guest, or prisoner, for nineteen years.

All this time when English seamen were chasing Spanish ships laden with bullion Elizabeth was equally non-committal, she neither praised nor punished her sailors, though her country was not (yet) at war with Spain, and these were hardly the acts of a friendly nation. But on one occasion when a sea-captain, Francis Drake, returned after a four-year voyage, she accepted an invitation to dine aboard his ship and knighted him on the deck. He had sailed round the world, the first Englishman to do so, and he had returned with Spanish treasure worth £800,000.

If the Spanish Ambassador at her Court complained, she always had her reply ready—a sharp reply, or teasing, or vague, according to her mood. The Ambassador would go away baffled; the acts of piracy continued.

SIR FRANCIS DRAKE
BEING KNIGHTED BY QUEEN ELIZABETH I

2

The Catholic–Protestant struggle intensified when the Pope released all Elizabeth's subjects from their duty of obedience to her. From then onwards Catholics in both England and Scotland regarded Mary as their true queen and Elizabeth as a usurper who ought to be deprived of her throne.

It was not safe to add "and her life" even when plotters thought they were alone, for Elizabeth was served by efficient spies whose chief knew exactly what was happening. Plots though there were, he exposed them when they had gone far enough, and none succeeded. Yet the Protestant Prince of Holland was assassinated, and Protestants in England had good reason to be apprehensive.

Only when a plot (Babington's) had been uncovered, which definitely involved Mary with Elizabeth's would-be assassins, was the English Queen at last compelled to make up her mind. Under strong pressure from her advisers, inch by inch she came, as if under torture, to that hateful, fateful decision—which she immediately recalled and cancelled, but too late, the word had gone out, the warrant was signed—that Mary must die. This decision was tremendous in its consequences, and impossible to take back.

From the moment of Mary's death a new vigour was seen in the preparations which were already begun, to send Spanish forces into England and put a Catholic monarch on the throne. These moves had been made more or less secretly but now they were in the open—it was war. The great fleet (Armada in Spanish) was to sail from Spain to the Netherlands and convey Philip's troops from there across to the Thames estuary. When all resistance was overcome Philip was to follow; when Elizabeth was dethroned, London—and then England—would welcome him as a Catholic king. Such was the plan.

England could make preparations too. Defences by sea and land were strengthened—ships, guns, stores, beacons and above all, men, were put in readiness.

When the Armada had been sighted and gunfire was sounding in the Channel, the land forces were assembled just north of the Thames at Tilbury, ready to move in any direction when the enemy attempted a landing. The Queen rode out to inspect them, and here are some of the words she spoke:

MY LOVING PEOPLE,

We have been persuaded by some, that are careful of our safety, to take heed how we commit ourselves to armed multitudes for fear of treachery; but I do assure you, I do not desire to live to distrust my faithful and loving people. Let tyrants fear: I have always so behaved myself that, under God, I have placed my chiefest strength and safeguard in the loyal hearts and good will of my subjects; and therefore I am come amongst you as you see at this time, not for my recreation and disport, but being resolved, in the midst and heat of the battle, to live or die amongst you all. . . .

One cannot doubt that the soldiers felt they would willingly die for her there and then; to them she *was* England. As we know now, the land forces were not needed that time; the conflict was fought out to a finish on the sea. England, Scotland and the Protestant cause in both countries were saved by Elizabeth's navy, with brilliant strategy and daring.

3

After 1588 Elizabeth's people, confident in their future, launched out on enterprises that belong to Commonwealth history rather than her own life-story.

But for her it was not a time of ease, though perhaps more free from crises and complications than before. The war with Spain was not yet officially ended, so there were still minor actions at sea. Ireland sheltered Jesuits and Spanish agents, and a major war had to be waged before the island was subdued; but France had peace within its own borders after a Protestant king came to the throne in 1589; he later became a Catholic and gave freedom of worship to all his subjects.

Elizabeth grew older and had to accustom herself to new faces and younger voices. When her Secretary died, his son Robert Cecil took his place. If complaints were heard in Parliament about her government, "Harry's daughter" knew how to give way and flatter the members without giving away too much.

She liked to be flattered herself, too. Restlessly energetic, she constantly travelled from one great house to another. Her dresses were magnificent. Sometimes (as at Elvetham, Hampshire) an elaborate pageant or musical show was staged for her. In 1601 she visited the Middle Temple, one of the lawyers' "Inns" in London. In its panelled hall may still be seen the table where she banqueted, a table made from timbers of the *Golden Hind* in which Drake had sailed round the world. Here she watched what was then a quite new play—this was its first performance—entitled *Twelfth Night, or What you Will*.

Watching a comedy, the Queen could laugh and put State matters aside for an hour or two, but at the time she was seriously troubled about one of her courtiers, Lord Essex. He had been given command of her army in Ireland; having disobeyed orders and been a failure over there, he returned and plotted rebellion against his Queen and Robert Cecil. She was obliged to let the law which decreed death for traitors, have its course. It was said that she never recovered from the distress of this affair as she had a great affection for Essex.

Although she would not discuss what should happen after her death, it was agreed by all concerned that King James VI of Scotland (Queen Mary's son, but a Protestant) should succeed. In him the crowns of Scotland and England would be united. When Queen Elizabeth died, after a few days' illness, all arrangements had been quietly made by Cecil, and James VI came south from Edinburgh to be crowned as James I of England.

CHAPTER FOURTEEN

James I: Charles I

I

In a certain picture in a collection called "High Hats", the first monarch of a united Great Britain is shown wearing a black hat, of ordinary width but looking quite fifteen inches high, a regular stove-pipe. In the portrait shown here, the object on the table at the right is also a hat, decked with soft high plumes. James could well be called, if not High Hat, a High Brow; he was extremely well-informed, well-read, talkative and clever. Those hats suited him.

His doublets were padded, not so much to make him look big and important, as to make them dagger-proof. He had been King of Scots since he was an infant, and three out of the four Regents in his minority had met violent deaths; he had known many nerve-racking moments in his own unquiet kingdom. All through life he could not bear loud or sudden noises.

Already married to the fair-haired Anne of Denmark, and father of two sons and a daughter, James came to the English court ready to be guided by Robert Cecil's advice. He made him Earl of Salisbury, but other less honourable courtiers gained influence over the King whose hands, as the picture shows, look soft and hang down in a limp and helpless way. He had not a statesman's grasp of affairs either at home or abroad.

James disliked the Presbyterian form of religion (in which he had been brought up) as much as he disliked "Popery", and therefore willingly continued Elizabeth's pattern of church organisation and worship; the theory he most strongly supported was that of the Divine Right of Kings. By the end of his reign, however, most of the extreme Protestants had left the Church of England; some had left England itself—for America. The only solid benefit to religion was the Authorised Version of the Bible, whose translators gratefully acknowledged that James had been the "chief mover" of their work.

James's daughter Elizabeth ("the Queen of Hearts") married the head of one of the German Protestant States. Her title was Electress

ANNO DNI · 1 5 4 4 ·

LADI MARI   DOVGHTER TO
THE MOST   VERTVOVS PRINCE
KINGE HENRI   THE EIGHT

THE AGE OF   XXVIII YERES

PLATE XI   MARY I

PLATE XII   ELIZABETH I

JAMES I *Daniel Mytens*

Charles I.st King of
Gr. Britain Fr. & Ireland.
N. 1600. M. 1640.

PLATE XIV   CHARLES I   *After Van Dyck*

Palatine, and she went to live in Heidelberg's castle of red stone above the River Neckar. Her father tried to gain support for his son-in-law in the struggle which was just then beginning between the Catholic and Protestant States—the Thirty Years War—but his efforts were fruitless.

When the House of Commons suggested what lines he ought to follow in dealing with foreign affairs, he told them it was not their business. They entered a protest in their Journal—freedom to discuss *any* topic being one of their privileges. James sent for the Journal and tore out that page.

He certainly wanted peace; his motto, he said, was "Blessed are the peacemakers", but he did not know how to make it happen.

Like the first Tudor king, the first Stuart king of England was grieved with the loss of a promising son and heir: James and Anne's elder son Henry died of typhoid fever at the age of eighteen. Prince Henry's room can still be seen in a house in the Strand (near Somerset House, once the residence of Edward VI's Protector) with panelling, carving and furniture of the style called after James "Jacobean".

2

Between Sovereign and Parliament today the relationship can be easily seen, literally seen by anyone with television, on such an occasion as the State opening of Parliament. On that day the Lords assemble in their House, the Commons are summoned and the Queen reads her Speech to them both, outlining her Ministers' plans for the coming session. For a short while the three are together under one roof, the inseparable three of our constitution—the Sovereign, the Lords and the Commons. Trumpets sound for her a loyal welcome and against a glittering background with scarlet and gold, diamonds and ermine, the traditional ceremony is performed; the scene is a reminder that this constitution is based not on written rules but on good understanding between Sovereign and People.

The tie has not always been close or kindly. Of all times in English history, the reign of Charles I showed King and Parliament furthest apart—actually at war. Then, there was pageantry of a different sort. Trumpets sounded for cavalry to charge, the scarlet was bloodshed, the glitter was sharp-edged steel.

Constitutional form may be important, wrote S. R. Gardiner, one of the foremost students of the Civil War, but "the character of governor and governed is of far greater importance". Charles inherited a relationship which was already unhappy; only a man of exceptional character could have put it right. His portraits show a man conscious of majesty, honourable, yet with a touch of scorn for people he did not understand. He faced a House of Commons full of rugged, determined characters, men who were sensitive in conscience and in pocket; not to be forced in matters of religion, and insistent on their rights in matters of taxation.

To start with, the House of Commons yielded to the King's wishes or he yielded to theirs, but reluctantly. Then for eleven years he ruled through his own officials without Parliament at all, but he angered the Scottish Presbyterians by consenting to Archbishop Laud's attempts to force upon them the rule of bishops. A Scottish army invaded northern England, and the emergency compelled Charles to summon a Parliament in 1640. The "Long" Parliament abolished the courts by means of which Charles had enforced his will, and condemned his chief Minister to death for treason. News reported from Ireland, of violent action by Catholics, heightened the tension in Parliament, especially as the King's wife (Henrietta Maria) was a Catholic. The split widened between the King's followers (Royalists) and the Parliamentarians (Roundheads). Early in 1642 both sides began to prepare for fighting. The Queen and the royal children were sent for safety to France, her country. Despite all efforts to prevent it, civil war broke out.

Four years later it ended with victory for Parliament, and the King a captive. But the victors themselves were disunited; the army officers and civilians formed two distinct factions. From his various prisons, by letters and messages, Charles tried to set off one against the other and bargain also with the Scots, to restore him to his kingly position. Then the parliamentary army officers seized the meeting-place at Westminster, turned out their opponents and set up a revolutionary court of justice to try Charles, feeling that he could never be trusted and should be deposed. Some thought the war had been entirely his fault and wanted him to die; and this opinion gained ground.

Westminster Hall was the scene of his trial. Charles sat in the middle facing the court; he wore black, with the blue ribbon and Order of the Garter. Throughout, he kept his temper and his dignity, but was given little chance to speak for himself, and no one there would defend him.

Finally he listened to the sentence pronouncing him guilty as a "Tyrant, Traytor, Murtherer and Publick Enemy".

THE TRIAL OF CHARLES I
AT WESTMINSTER HALL

He faced his end calmly, saying, "Death is not terrible to me; I bless God, I am prepared", and on the morning fixed, January 29th, 1649, he walked to the executioner's block, just outside his own palace of Whitehall, and knelt down, sure of his innocence to the last. The axe was lifted, and then with a single blow the kingdoms of England, Scotland and Ireland were left without a king.

The warrant condemning Charles had been signed by fifty-nine names, of which the first was J. Bradshaw (a lawyer who had presided at the trial), and the third was O. Cromwell.

CHAPTER FIFTEEN

Charles II : James II

I

Oliver Cromwell became the most powerful man in England, which he governed from 1653 until his death in 1658.

Charles, the eldest son of Charles I, was in exile abroad for most of the years of civil war and non-royal rule. He and the Royalists considered that his reign had begun at the instant his father died; he was only waiting for the right moment, to come back and be crowned. Not until after Oliver Cromwell's death and some months of confusion that followed it, did that moment come.

Before leaving Holland where he had been living, Charles promised to forgive past injuries, only excepting those men who had actually condemned his father to death. He also promised "liberty to tender consciences". He landed at Dover on his thirtieth birthday and was uproariously welcomed all the way to London, while in country and town the people expressed their delight with bells ringing, bonfires blazing, beer flowing and such songs as "Here's a health unto His Majesty!"

Charles was the son of a French mother, and had spent all those years abroad, yet he well understood the nation to which he had returned. The hardships of his exile had not embittered him, only he felt now, obviously, that nothing mattered much, so long as he was not sent into exile again. His first Parliament was very hard on people who did not completely conform to the Church of England, yet Charles let them be persecuted—and put his promise to tender consciences in the background—rather than displease the House of Commons. They held the purse-strings, and he, though not extravagant, never had any surplus money and seldom even enough.

The King was easy-going, affable; people would treasure a smile from him or a recognising nod, and long remember his witty, sometimes cynical remarks. He led a life of pleasure, and although fond of his wife (Catherine, who was Portuguese) he quite openly neglected her for other ladies, an example which, like the Plague of 1665, was as infectious as it was corrupting. The Lord Chancellor Clarendon, a God-

fearing man who had served the King's father and himself faithfully for years, protested. He was mocked behind his back, as being old-fashioned; the laughter so often heard in the Merry Monarch's court was not always free from malice. In 1667 the Chancellor, who had made many people angry, was dismissed. His new house outside London, just finished, was never lived in; he retired to Paris. Yet his family name, Hyde, is often on the lips of Londoners, who call the estate round that house, Hyde Park.

Meanwhile in St. James's Palace the King made artists, actors, musicians and scientists all feel at home. He had a keen appreciation of the arts, and gave the Royal Society its charter. Two theatres were built with the "picture-frame" stage which was then new. In leisure hours Charles liked to stroll in the grounds, chat with friends, watch the ducks and inspect trees he had planted. A strange animal "between a greyhound and a spaniel" was one devoted companion; he also had other, well-bred little dogs.

A terrifying emergency in the year after the Plague showed Charles in a different light, still unperturbed, but prompt, practical and plucky. The Great Fire of London raged for six days, the Mayor could not prevent panic and was himself exhausted, but Charles and his brother the Duke of York organised rescue work and got boats to take away the people and such goods as they could save.

When London was a plain of black ruins and hot ashes, Charles quickly got in touch with his surveyor-general, Sir Christopher Wren, who within four days had sketched plans for re-building the city. His scheme as a whole was not used, but Wren designed the new St Paul's Cathedral besides fifty-two other churches, thirty-six halls, the Custom-house, the Monument and several private houses. All through the next years London was being re-built. In 1682 Wren built for Charles the Home for veteran soldiers, Chelsea Hospital, which in its purpose though not its ground-plan, resembled the Hôtel des Invalides in Paris.

91

2

One king, only, occupied the throne of France from 1643 to 1715. The reign of Louis XIV was unequalled, not only in its long duration. His court was a magnet, drawing to itself the talent, culture and wealth of France; and a model, for other courts to copy.

Louis XIV, nephew of Henrietta Maria and therefore a first cousin of Charles II and his brothers and sisters, was an absolute monarch, unchecked by any parliament and able to impose his will on his subjects. He was a Catholic, who desired to see all his subjects Catholics likewise. He believed that the area of France ought to be extended to the limits made for her by Nature, i.e. from the Pyrenees to the Rhine; any part not yet included in the French kingdom would be put there sooner or later by the highly-trained French army and the genius of her military commanders.

Charles saw nothing outrageous in these aims of France, and tried to steer England accordingly. He married the Portuguese princess mainly because Portugal was allied with France. He kept contact with the French Court through his sister the Duchess of Orleans, to whom he was devoted; he used to write to her daily. But when it was known that Charles had agreed with Louis, in return for money, to join in war against Protestant Holland, and adding a secret clause that he, Charles, would declare himself a Catholic at a suitable moment—naturally some English politicians felt uneasy. They formed an opposition without going so far as to let themselves be suspected of treason.

Lord Shaftesbury founded a club whose members, wearing a green ribbon, used to meet in a tavern beside Temple Bar. They wanted (1) to restrain Charles from tying England too closely to French schemes, and (2) to ensure that his brother, known to be a Catholic, should not succeed to the throne. The green ribbon wearers were nicknamed Whigs—meaning sour-faced hypocrites—by the King's friends; they retorted by calling the Court party Tories, meaning wild rapscallions.

Charles moved adroitly between the two factions, and accepted from his French cousin sums of money which made it unnecessary to ask Parliament for grants; in his last four years he had no Parliament at all.

He cleverly kept the politicians in good humour, and was popular to the last. On his death-bed he was received into the Roman Catholic Church. He left open for his brother, who *was* to succeed him in spite of the Whigs, various pitfalls which he himself had managed to avoid.

3

James, Duke of York, three years younger than Charles II, had shared in the rough wandering life of the royal family. Aged fifteen, he had escaped from St James's Palace dressed as a girl, and fled overseas. He had served in the French army and been praised by a famous French general. When his brother was restored to the throne, James as Lord High Admiral did much to improve the British Navy.

His strong family likeness can be seen—the long nose, the arched eyebrows—but his colouring was fairer than that of Charles, who as a child had been nicknamed the Black Boy.

James turned Roman Catholic about 1670 after his first wife Anne had done so, but both their daughters Mary and Anne remained Protestant. (Mary married the Stadholder of Holland, William of Orange, while Anne married a Danish prince named George.) James's wife Anne died in 1671 and he took as his second wife an Italian Catholic princess, Mary Beatrice of Modena.

In the year of James's accession to the throne (1685) Louis XIV withdrew from his Protestant subjects the freedom and protection they had hitherto enjoyed. In the persecutions that followed, many took refuge in England and their piteous stories filled English Protestants with horror and the fear that the like might happen to *them* under a Catholic king.

One Protestant rebellion in Scotland, and another in south-west England, were both easily quelled by James and his very success encouraged him to act openly in favour of his fellow-Catholics. He increased his permanent army to 30,000 men and stationed half of them in a camp near London, thus making the Londoners feel they were being watched and overawed. He appointed Catholics as officers, in defiance of a law passed only a few years before. He made other Catholic appointments. Oxford, hitherto most loyal to the Stuart family, now turned against James, because if he could cancel a law like that, or "suspend" it, or "dispense" with it, what was to stop him from doing the same with every one of the laws, just as it suited him? Englishmen may well have felt that all the parliamentary struggle and the Civil War, which some could remember, had been for nothing and they would soon be back in the bad old days of King John—especially as they knew there was a highly successful absolute monarch just across the Channel.

It was the failure to imagine, recognise or allow for such natural fears, rather than anything intentionally wicked in James, that ended his reign so speedily.

All the feelings of discontent and dread came to the surface in the summer of 1688. Early in June the King ordered that a Declaration should be read in churches giving freedom of worship to all. However sensible and Christian the idea may seem to us now, at the time it was seen as a step towards Popery—because it included the Catholics! Seven Bishops begged the King to withdraw his orders, as being contrary to law. The Bishops were perfectly correct, but they were imprisoned in the Tower.

On June 10th, Queen Mary Beatrice gave birth to a son. An heir for the King! But if the Catholics were pleased, the Protestants were glum, because now the Crown, on James's death, would not go to his Protestant daughter Mary (the Princess of Orange), but to this infant, who of course would grow up in the faith held by his parents.

Meanwhile the seven Bishops were tried, on a charge of seditious libel. The jury found them not guilty, and on July 1st they were released. The Londoners shouted for joy, and even the army encamped on Hounslow Heath cheered them as seven heroes.

But the nation had been badly scared. Immediately and secretly a letter signed by seven Protestant leaders (three Whigs and four Tories), was sent to the Prince of Orange asking him to come to Britain with a force, and protect the rights of the Protestant Church, and of his wife Mary. It assured him that nineteen-twentieths of the people would support him.

William judged that Britain would be a useful ally to him in defending Holland. He said "Now or never", and accepted the proposals. By the end of October he was ready and on 5th November he landed with his soldiers at Brixham in Devon, and began to march towards London.

James found that his army was deserting him and going over to William's side. Although his earlier career had proved him no coward, he could not face the shame and finality of a formal handing-over of kingship, and he decided to escape. As he was rowed out in a boat on the Thames, to board the larger ship that was to take him to France, the fugitive King threw into the water the Great Seal, the symbol of authority, and from that moment he was considered to have ceased to reign.

PLATE XV   CHARLES II   *J. M. Wright*

PLATE XVI   JAMES II

PLATE XVII   WILLIAM III   *After Sir Peter Lely*

PLATE XVIII   MARY II   *After William Wissing*

CHAPTER SIXTEEN

William III and Mary II: Anne

I

James did not intend his exit to be a final one. He hoped to regain his kingdom. He was like a man chased out of his house through the front door; if he cannot re-enter that way he will try the side door, or the back. James still had hopes of returning through Ireland or Scotland.

Meanwhile, with all proper legal forms, William and Mary became King and Queen, equal in sovereignty. Mary crossed from The Hague early in 1689, and they were crowned in April. At long last, the limits between royal power and parliamentary claims were set down in the Bill of Rights and generally accepted. Hence the events of 1688–89 are called the Glorious Revolution. The liberty of subjects had been secured without bloodshed.

The Toleration Act soon followed, allowing non-members of the Church of England free worship (though they still could not hold responsible posts such as that of mayor, or officer in the armed forces). In Scotland the equivalent amount of toleration was granted; in Ireland it was promised, but was in fact not given, so the Catholics went on being penalised.

Scattered over the three kingdoms James had his supporters, called Jacobites. ("James" is "Jacobus" in Latin.) It is a mistake to think they were all Scottish Highlanders. Yet it was at Killiecrankie in Perthshire that a battle was fought on his behalf. The Jacobite leader was killed here, and this first blow for James in Scotland was not followed up; the majority really wanted William and Mary.

His back-door attempt to get into England having failed, James resolved to try the side door, and went over to Ireland himself. As the vast majority of Irish were Catholics, the situation looked more promising; but "Orange Billy" proved himself an able general and outmatched James in a swift summer campaign, of which his victory at the River Boyne was the triumphant climax and is still celebrated by Protestants in Northern Ireland on its anniversary. After it James retreated to France and tried no more, though he and every Jacobite continued to regard William as a usurper. James lived in the palace put at his disposal by Louis XIV, and died there in 1701. Mary Beatrice lived on for many years.

The victorious forty-year-old general who sat in his saddle for nineteen hours (and received a wound as well) at the Battle of the Boyne was no handsome and dashing Cavalier; there was nothing romantic about William, though his toughness and endurance cannot be questioned. He had little physical strength, being short, thin, asthmatic, anaemic and in later life, tuberculous in one lung. But what willpower! His face, marked with smallpox, was seldom seen to smile, but the eyes were piercing and keen. Since his early twenties William had borne the burden of ruling and defending his country, and he had confronted French generals who were immensely more formidable than his father-in-law, ex-King James.

Defence of the Netherlands, the main task of William's life, required both war and diplomacy. By persuasion, in which his perfect command of four languages and understanding of three others played a useful part, he had managed to build up a great alliance of European States to withstand French attacks. As the War of the Grand Alliance was being waged from 1688 to 1697, naturally William could not spare much time to be in England.

When he *was* there, the smoke and fogs of London in winter were so bad for his health that he preferred to live at Hampton Court, partially re-built for him by Wren, or at a new palace at Kensington, modelled in brown brick on his country house near The Hague. William and Mary's Dutch garden at Kensington still delights the eye with its formal flower-beds, the water-lilies and the walk that passes beneath cunningly twined branches of lime-trees.

2

At Kensington, Queen Mary would see the Dutch gardeners at work; she could speak to them in their language, and she loved flowers. Indoors, she never liked being idle, and she read a great deal, or when this hurt her eyes she would take up some needlework and ask someone else to read aloud. In company, though William was apt to be silent, his wife talked enough for two, but it was not mere empty gossip; she had a lively, active mind.

Mary was too modest to think she counted much in public affairs, but when William was away she took full charge: she hated scandal and

immorality, and made her appointments with care. Always she was loyal to her husband, and though her father was politically their enemy, she would never allow him to be spoken of disrespectfully. Her position was not at all an easy one. Amid all her anxieties she constantly read the Bible, and spent much time praying.

When this lovable, warm-hearted Queen was carried off at the age of thirty-two—by the very same disease, smallpox, which William had once come through—his grief was overwhelming. He was always thought "reserved", and had few friends. He had not always treated Mary kindly, and realised then as perhaps never before, how unselfish she was. William founded in her memory the Naval Hospital at Greenwich, a project which she had already set her heart on, but had not been able to bring about. Also, there had been a coldness between the royal couple and Princess Anne. William and his sister-in-law now became reconciled.

William's balance of failure and success in the war had been fairly even. England had never taken to him very kindly as a person, but the Whigs at least backed him in the Continental struggle. In 1697 a peace was arranged, by which the French kept most of their conquests, but William could put Dutch garrisons into a row of fortresses to guard the Netherlands frontier.

This was only a breathing-space. Another war was not far off and William might have had a major part in it, but death intervened. While riding at Hampton Court he was thrown from his horse which had stumbled over a molehill, and his collar-bone was broken. His diseased lung became inflamed. Worn already by fatigue and strain, he died a few days later.

Parliament had already provided that if he and Mary died without heirs, the succession should go to Princess Anne.

3

"Queen Anne" has become an adjective. There are Queen Anne chairs, Queen Anne spoons, Queen Anne mirrors and so on. These are always beautiful things of a recognisable style, valued by collectors. They happen to have been made in her reign but have little or nothing to do with *her*; only England was fortunate enough then to have good designers and craftsmen. Tea (pronounced "tay") was becoming a fashionable drink, sipped from small, delicate, handle-less cups; elegance in dress and manners went along with the tea drinking. Of a certain great house, the poet Alexander Pope wrote:

> "Here thou, great Anna, whom three realms obey,
> Dost sometimes counsel take, and sometimes tea."

Queen Anne had pretty hands and a pleasant voice—she had been taught by an actress how to speak. Her friendships and dislikes were rather violent, but she was not original or remarkable in any way, nor was her husband. They had a number of children, who all died young. The eldest was William, and William III was his godfather. The Dutch King, having no children of his own, was fond of the little boy, and many hopes were centred on him, but he died at the age of eleven.

Queen Anne's reign was a stirring time in the history of the nation. The struggle to prevent France from dominating Europe continued, and Marlborough carried on where William III left off.

To prevent aid to the French coming from (or through) Scotland, the Whig leaders in both England and Scotland decided on an important move. The Scottish Parliament was to be abolished and Scotland would have, instead, representatives in the English one. Thus Britain would present a single front to the world. With safeguards for Scotland's freedom of action in her law-courts, churches and schools, and with financial compensation from the richer country to the poorer one, the proposals were accepted. In consequence of this Union (1707) two out of "great Anna's" "three realms" were going to act together, and as the wars with France were by no means over, the regiments, ships and resources of Britain were going to be needed in all parts of the globe.

CHAPTER SEVENTEEN

George I: George II

I

Between the royal Stuart line and the Hanoverians, the connecting link was a marriage, celebrated half-way through the seventeenth century. The bridegroom was the ruling prince of Hanover. The bride was Sophia, called the Merry Debonaire, twelfth of the thirteen children of the Elector and Electress Palatine. The latter (mentioned on p. 82) was Elizabeth, the beautiful and attractive daughter of James I. She, although most of her life was spent on the Continent, was born in Scotland and died in England. Her daughter Sophia, then, was joined with the Hanoverian line and this couple, both Protestants, were the parents of George, who was born in the city of Hanover.

The connection through his British grandmother was slight; George was German in his outlook. He was already in the mid-fifties when Queen Anne's death added to his Electoral title the royal British one. Of his previous life little need be said. He had been in the wars and "liked fighting better than learning". He had married his cousin the Princess of Celle, but their marriage broke up and their two children stayed with grandparents. The boy was the future George II; the girl, the future Queen of Prussia. After about 1700 George must have known that his future lay in Britain, a country he had only once briefly visited; but although he was industrious in governing Hanover—and although he could speak French fluently—he never learned English.

He would not have been a typical German prince, without a good ear and a cultivated musical taste. His Kapellmeister was G. F. Handel, who visited London in 1712, and stayed there. On arriving in England in 1714, George was displeased with the composer for outstaying his leave, and refused to see him; but Handel cleverly regained his master's favour, aided by an English friend and a Hanoverian one. The new King and his party were to travel one day down the Thames from Whitehall to Limehouse. Handel's friends hired a barge to follow behind the royal one, and in it a small orchestra was playing a suite that Handel had just written. The sound of these lovely airs

wafted over the water so enchanted the King that he asked who the composer was, and when Handel's name was given, his anger melted away. Such was the origin of the well-known "Water Music", according to tradition. Handel was naturalised and as "Composer to the Court" he continued active into the reign of George II.

George I let the members of his Cabinet Council—the heads of departments—discuss State matters among themselves, without worrying too much if he did not understand what was said. Sir Robert Walpole is usually reckoned as the first of the Prime Ministers; from 1721 onwards he presided at these meetings, and gradually the King stopped coming, though he and Walpole sometimes managed to talk together in Latin.

Unfortunately George I and his son could not get on with each other. Because of the known dislike between them and also because the King's large household was thought to cost too much, George was never popular.

It was different in Hanover. He used to visit his native country about every other year, and his subjects there were delighted to see him. On one of these journeys towards Hanover, travelling in his coach through Holland, he had a stroke, from which he never recovered.

2

When the son of George I knew that he would inherit Britain's Crown he came to visit his future realm, and was given by Queen Anne various titles that have a rare English flavour about them, like Baron Tewkesbury, and Viscount Northallerton. Later, he commanded troops in Marlborough's army and was in the thick of the battle of Oudenarde, where he led a cavalry charge and repeatedly risked his life.

After his father's accession George was still proud to be one of the English and to speak their language, although he never lost his German accent. He went on gathering honours; he was, of course, Prince of Wales, and appeared as chief guest at the Lord Mayor's banquet in London, and even achieved the degree of D.D. at Cambridge. We do not *know* that he gave up eating Wurst and Sauerkraut in favour of roast beef and Yorkshire pudding, but that would have been in his line. "I have not," he once said, "a drop of blood in my veins which is not English." As a statement of course this was untrue, but as an expression of goodwill to England it was very acceptable.

The portrait here given (p. 109) rather tones down the colouring with which George II is described in his youth: large blue eyes, a reddish-purple complexion, fair hair and eyebrows. He was small and neat, and held himself rather stiffly—he strutted and posed and liked being in the limelight.

George's wife was the flaxen-haired Caroline of Ansbach. He used to fall in love rather easily with other women, but Caroline was not jealous by nature, she understood him well and would readily forgive. They had three daughters—taught music when they were children by Handel—and two sons, Frederick and William. Here the story of George I repeats itself, as Frederick could not abide his parents and there were bitter family quarrels with faults on both sides. Frederick died before his father, leaving one son who eventually succeeded to the throne.

The courage George had shown at Oudenarde was displayed again when as a man of sixty he led his troops at the battle of Dettingen in 1743. He was the last British sovereign to take part in a battle.

George was impulsive and irritable, and could have involved Britain in war more than once, but as long as Walpole remained minister the strongest influence was for peace. The King chafed under Walpole's restraint but was sincerely grateful for his service, and when the twenty-one years of Walpole's ministry ended, George wept on parting with him.

George II visited Hanover hardly less often than his father, whether in war or peace. When Britain was at war with France and Prussia, the Jacobites supported James II's grandson in an attempt to gain the throne. At one point it looked as if they might succeed; there was panic in London, but George kept cool, and the moment passed. When the Stuart prince, advancing from the north, had got the length of Derby, he was advised to retreat, and came no further. The King's son, William, Duke of Cumberland, conducted the campaign against him with savagery, but with success, and within the next four months it was all over.

> "Burned are our homes, exile and death
> Scatter the loyal men,
> Yet ere the sword cool in the sheath
> Charlie will come again!"

The last two lines of that Jacobite song are merely wishful thinking, for "Charlie" never did come again, and the Hanoverian dynasty was established more firmly than ever.

By far the greatest English statesman in George's latter years was William Pitt, afterwards Earl of Chatham. George thought that he underrated Hanover's importance, but Pitt's mind reached out to the future for Britain in distant colonies, in sea-power and in the markets of the world. War against France, renewed in 1756, began with disastrous losses to Britain. The next year, public demand compelled the King, who had distrusted Pitt, to place him at the head of affairs. "Give me your confidence," Pitt said to George, "and I will deserve it." "Deserve my confidence," was the reply, "and you shall have it."

Pitt was a great organiser of victory and the situation completely changed, in Asia, in North America, on the seas and in Europe. But before peace could be concluded or even thought of, George died one morning of heart-failure at the age of seventy-seven.

PLATE XIX   ANNE   *J. Closterman*

PLATE XX   GEORGE I   *Studio of Sir Godfrey Kneller*

PLATE XXI   GEORGE II   *T. Worlidge*

PLATE XXII   GEORGE III   *Studio of Allan Ramsay*

CHAPTER EIGHTEEN

George III

I

A slow, dense boy who could not concentrate, who could only read when he was eleven, and whose handwriting remained childish, lost his father when he was thirteen. Naturally the boy depended on his mother for advice, and felt the need of a man to take his father's place.

The boy who became King George III when he was twenty-two, was so placed, and so trained. The Earl of Bute (a Tory) was his tutor and became his unofficial adviser. Both Bute and the boy's mother, the Princess of Wales, impressed on George that the Whig party and its land-owning families had ruled for long enough; when he was king he must *be* a king, he must make his own decisions and rule through men of his own choosing.

George kept their instructions in mind. One of his first actions as King was to seek a wife. Princess Charlotte of Mecklenburg-Strelitz was chosen. Her parents having approved the match, the small, pale, plain-looking Princess was fetched from her Baltic homeland to become George's Queen. She was a loyal, affectionate consort and they led a simple life quietly in their homes either at Richmond or in the house which George bought near St James's Palace, called Buckingham House, in 1762.

George came to the throne in war-time just after the "wonderful year" of victories, and made Lord Bute his chief Minister, not realising his unfitness for such a post. George disliked the men who were already directing the war; and habitually he chose the *person* he felt dependable, rather than one whose *policy* would benefit the nation. Eager to end the war quickly, he approved suggested peace terms which would have given France many advantages, *too* many, thought Pitt, who had done so much to achieve the previous year's triumphs. Pitt, backed by the City merchants, denounced the proposed peace terms (for three and a half hours!) in the House of Commons.

Outside, Pitt was cheered by crowds when he appeared in public, whereas George's coach was watched with hostile groans and hisses.

The London mob, who hated Bute for being "Scotch" as well as incompetent, paraded the streets holding aloft two poles, one with a petticoat fastened to it (to signify the influence of George's mother) and the other, a boot—a wretched pun on Bute's name; they could not bear either him or the lady, and burned both the objects in a bonfire.

George obstinately pursued his plans and finally persuaded his Paymaster, in return for a peerage (he became Lord Holland) to bribe every M.P. he could reach, to vote in favour of the Peace. So it was carried, and the Seven Years War ended. "Now my son is King of England!" cried the delighted Dowager-Princess, but she alone was pleased. Bute, unable to endure all the scorn heaped on him, soon resigned.

George was still not confident in himself—he had a spell of insanity in 1765—and tried to gain Pitt's friendship, making him Earl of Chatham, but the Earl was in poor health and only able to give George fitful support. Moreover, their views about the colonies in America were opposite from the outset. George found many supporters in Parliament who believed that at this time the King should take a more active part in affairs, noticing daily how each man spoke and voted, and rewarding and promoting those who did as he wanted. They became a political force and were called the King's Friends, but this did not end corruption nor banish party strife.

Worse difficulties were to follow. After many crises and several changes of Ministry George appointed in 1770 the Tory Lord North, a man who agreed with him entirely and was as unlike Chatham as a rubber sponge is unlike a granite rock. North was lazy and would sleep during speeches in Parliament. George worked hard, mastering the business of the government departments, instructing North what line to take in debates and so on. While gifted men were wasting their talents in opposition, the King and North were directing the moves which eventually goaded the American colonists into revolt. On the very brink of war, however, they sent no more British soldiers to America, while they actually reduced the number of sailors in the Navy.

George's attitude to the colonists throughout was that in everything they must obey the Mother country, and if not, they were rebels; whereas Chatham had exclaimed "Sir, I rejoice that America has resisted!"

No one doubts that George was sincere, yet when every excuse has been made—and the Whigs did not help the King—it has to be said that he and Lord North were to blame for the colonies breaking away; and having let war begin, they conducted it so badly that Britain's former enemies—France, Spain, Holland—joined in, which made Britain's defeat certain. Chatham died before it was half-way through.

2

By the end of the War of American Independence George was no longer self-distrustful; he had gained experience and was more than ever convinced that he knew best. But Lord North, conscious of failure, resigned even before peace-terms were settled.

After trying out various ministries, none of which lasted long, George surprised the politicians by choosing for Prime Minister the son of Chatham, William Pitt the Younger. This twenty-four-year-old Cambridge graduate was to revive and modernise the Tory party's ideas, and to steer Britain through another life-and-death struggle with France, not the old France governed by kings, but the new France of the Revolution.

Meanwhile the King and Queen were harassed by family troubles. Their sons were becoming notorious for bad behaviour. The eldest (later the Prince Regent and then George IV) was friendly with the Whig leader Charles Fox, a reckless gambler; the Prince was deep in debt. In 1788 the King had another attack of his mental illness. The Prince was to have acted as Regent, but the King's recovery after a few months made it needless.

By this time the disasters of the American war were largely forgotten and George was not so low in public esteem. The Prince's wild conduct and the King's displeasure were well known, and won him some sympathy. He was heartily cheered when he drove to St Paul's Cathedral to give thanks for his recovery. Then, when the French revolutionaries imprisoned their King and royal family and sent them to be guillotined, the horror felt in Britain was genuine and increased the sense of loyalty to the throne.

One belief that George clung to through thick and thin, mad or sane, was that he as a Protestant must never give or allow any concession to Roman Catholics. To do so, he was convinced, would be to break his coronation oath. This fixed idea put Pitt in a terrible dilemma just at the time when the war to prevent French Revolutionary ideas from spreading, was becoming a war to defend this island against invasion by Napoleon Bonaparte.

Knowing that the French could use Ireland as a base for invading England, Pitt proposed to unite the Irish Parliament with that of England; hoping to induce the Irish to agree, he had given the Catholics to understand they would be freed from every disability under which they had been forced to live for centuries. The emancipation of Catholics was long overdue, and was bound to come (it did come in 1829). George III utterly and completely refused it in 1800. The Union of the Parliaments was managed, but with an astonishing amount of bribery. Pitt felt bound to resign, and the King went mad under the strain.

Pitt died in 1806 and the war against Napoleon continued, but George was failing, and knew not when it had reached its end. He grieved so much over a beloved daughter's death in 1810 that he lost his sanity in 1811 and this time he never regained it. Throughout this period the Prince of Wales (later George IV) acted as Regent.

During the earlier bouts George III had been physically healthy, but in these last years he lost his sight and hearing, and wandered like a ghost around the rooms in Windsor Castle where he was confined, a pitiable sight indeed with his ragged white hair and beard, and clad in his purple dressing-gown—playing the harpsichord sometimes, and constantly talking, to people who were not there.

CHAPTER NINETEEN

George IV : William IV

I

England has had kings who were perhaps more wicked than the sons of George III, yet respect for the Crown has seldom sunk so low as in the lifetime of George IV.

It was not merely because he burdened his father's life, and distressed his mother beyond measure. That was the pattern of the Hanoverian reigns. The heir was constantly in opposition and rallied his party round him; it must have been easy to rebel against a man so sure of his own rightness as George III. As the father had learned from a Tory textbook and preferred Tory ministers, naturally the son lined up with the Whigs, though that did not prevent him disputing with them and deserting to the Tories after 1811, when his father was no longer there to be thwarted.

Nor was George IV despised merely because he was a gambler, spendthrift, heavy drinker and wrecker of women's honour. That was the character of the age, when marriage vows were lightly broken, and the phrase "as drunk as a lord" passed into the English language. But the fact that everybody else is doing it, has never yet made a wrong thing right, and by 1820 the nation's conscience had heard some rousing voices and was by no means asleep.

In 1795 George, then Prince of Wales, married Caroline of Brunswick. He had already been married ten years earlier to Mrs Fitzherbert, a Catholic widow, who honourably refused to give up her Catholic faith. Had this first marriage been known George would, by law, have lost his chance of inheriting the throne, so it was kept dark, but was one of those "secrets" that most people knew. On Caroline's arrival he repudiated and repulsed Mrs Fitzherbert—only to treat Caroline later in just the same way. She had one child, Charlotte, but George forbade the mother and child to see each other. Caroline never forgave him. Wild and wayward she may have been, but the nation's sympathy was on her side. These two wives were not the only women who lived with him for a time, and were cast off when he tired of them.

BRIGHTON PAVILION
IN THE EARLY NINETEENTH CENTURY

It is possible, and has been done, to write admiringly of George IV and condone his lapses, to emphasise his charm, and recall how kind he was to his servants, how affable to his guests. What brilliant parties he gave! How expert he was on wine and cookery, what unerring taste he showed in his furnishings and dress, how he praised artists, bought their pictures, enjoyed Jane Austen's novels and spoke graciously to Sir Walter Scott! There was elegance too in the buildings of the time, in Carlton House where he lived (on £60,000 a year, though he never made ends meet) and Buckingham Palace (his father's Buckingham House rebuilt). Especially elegant was Regent Street, with its beautiful curve; while the Pavilion at Brighton was in its flamboyant way a masterpiece.

True enough. Yet in the social history of the times poverty stands out in such glaring contrast to wealth, no one could be blind to it except a self-absorbed man to whom "out of sight" means "out of mind". Ragged ex-soldiers tramping from town to town looking for work and finding none; underfed labourers forced to poach in the woods to save their children from starving; and their desperate, famished women-folk—these were also George's subjects, and might have lived in another planet for all he cared; they were not likely to be impressed with the beautiful curve of Regent Street.

An ambassador's wife, who was often one of his guests, has left her impressions of George, and evidently, though she liked him, she was quite clear-sighted. He was a good mimic, she says, "he has some wit and great penetration . . . he knew how to listen, was very polished . . . he was very affectionate, sympathetic and gallant". She further says that he was full of vanity, and that no one trusted him.

2

William, Duke of Clarence, the next surviving son of George III, had been sent into the Navy when he was fourteen and served for ten years, coming through several naval actions and one battle. He knew Nelson well and admired him; the bullet that killed the great Admiral at Trafalgar was given by the surgeon afterwards to William, who kept it as long as he lived.

George IV's only child Charlotte died in 1817. This made William the heir to the throne, and not until then did he marry. A lady who had kept his house and was the mother of his children, had never been married to him; she had to leave. He chose as the future Queen, Princess Adelaide of Saxe-Meiningen, who shared his own liking for a quiet, simple country life. When George IV died they went to live at Windsor. Here she had a model dairy, and took a friendly interest in the estate workers, in fact the ways of this royal pair resembled those of George III ("Farmer George") and Queen Charlotte, much more than those of the late master of Carlton House.

They were obliged to cut down expenditure anyway, because of the late King's vast debts. Their coronation was not nearly so grand as people expected and was called by some witty (and probably disappointed) Londoner, a Half-a-Crownation. It actually cost about one-eighth of the previous one.

William also inherited from his brother an enormous back-log of routine work that had been left on one side—papers, literally thousands of them, that needed the royal signature; and the new King, aged 65, sat hour after hour patiently signing, with a bowl of hot water beside him, dipping his fingers in sometimes to relieve the pain, for he had rheumatism in his hands.

Wellington, the hero of the Peninsular War and victor of Waterloo, was William's first (Tory) Prime Minister, but soon gave place to Earl Grey and the Whigs, who were pledged to change the House of Commons, to make it more accurately represent the people, and to give voting power to the middle class. Proposals embodying this policy in a Reform Bill (the first one) passed their first reading in the Commons by one vote only, and at the next stage were rejected. A second Reform

Bill, passed wholly by the Commons, was thrown out by the Lords.
The country was in a ferment, and a possible civil war was spoken of
quite openly. Finally the King, who did not want to use unfair pressure
but saw how urgently Reform was needed, consented to promise
peerages to supporters of the third Bill and thus ensure its passage
through the Lords. He did not need to: as soon as this was known the
Bill's opponents withdrew and so it passed and became law in 1832.
The new, reformed Parliament was able to go forward to do some
most valuable work and, furthermore, a long step had been taken
towards "government of the people, by the people, for the people".

William was friendly and informal with the people of London. He
and Queen Adelaide went down the Thames in their royal barge to
open what was then the new London Bridge and sat at a banquet on
the bridge with the Lord Mayor, in full view of many citizens. It is to
William also that we owe permission to enter the royal parks. Before
his time they were the sovereign's private gardens, but he opened them
up for the public.

W.R. IV 1833

can be seen wrought in the iron entrance-gates to Wellington Barracks,
in Birdcage Walk.

He did not often drive in State, and had not much dignity of bearing.
He was apt to fuss, and swear, and get excited about trifles; he constantly repeated himself, and easily lost his temper, but at home he was
seen at his best as a kindly host. Queen Adelaide too was hospitable
and loved having children to stay at Windsor, the King's relations and
hers. Their own two little girls both died in infancy.

Only one of the children who might have been at these parties was
seldom seen, namely William's niece Victoria. She was passing her
rather solitary childhood at Kensington Palace. Her absence was in no
way the wish of the Princess herself, but due to the hatred between
King William and his sister-in-law (Victoria's mother) the Duchess of
Kent. This lady had strong likes and dislikes and would not let Victoria,
her only child, go near Windsor Castle.

But by the time Victoria was eleven, everybody, including Victoria
herself, knew that the Duchess of Kent's child was next in the line of
succession to the throne.

PLATE XXIII   GEORGE IV   *Sir Thomas Lawrence*
                                        Sketch in oils

PLATE XXIV   WILLIAM IV

PLATE XXV   VICTORIA   *Sir George Hayter*

PLATE XXVI   EDWARD VII   *Sir Luke Fildes*

CHAPTER TWENTY

Victoria

I

Photography was invented in Queen Victoria's reign, but it is not pictures that tell most about her. It is what she wrote herself. From the age of thirteen she kept a Journal, continued with few breaks till her death. She wrote hundreds of letters, many of which were kept. Thus she can be personally known as few other sovereigns have been. Further, her most outstanding trait was her truthfulness. As a small child, even a naughty one, Victoria never told lies, nor did she hide her feelings as she grew older. A frank, open nature, detesting humbug, clearly stands out in her writings and in other people's recorded impressions.

She was trained in childhood mainly by three people: her mother the Duchess of Kent, her governess Baroness Lehzen and her uncle Leopold (her mother's brother). Religious instruction was carefully given and in addition, when they knew Victoria was the future Queen, her mother took much trouble to devise a system of education that would equip the child for her life's work.

Baroness Lehzen (with some other instructors) carried it out, and to her fell the task of training the little girl in manners and behaviour. At first rebellious, Victoria grew fond of her and willingly did as she was told. When the eleven-year-old Princess learned that she would be queen some day, she first flushed and shed some tears—it was a shock—but then spoke quite sensibly to her governess about the splendour and the difficulties that lay ahead, and said, "I will be good."

Her uncle had lived at Claremont in Surrey with his wife, George IV's daughter Charlotte, and after the latter's death he continued to live there alone. Often he visited Kensington Palace, and as her own father had died when she was a baby, "Uncle Leopold" seemed like a father. When he left England to become King of the Belgians, he used to write long affectionate letters from Brussels, giving his niece advice.

He also, with Victoria's mother, laid plans for the girl's marriage. They arranged visits for various boy cousins, any of whom might have been suitable. When she was seventeen the two brother Princes, Ernest and Albert of Saxe-Coburg, stayed a while at Kensington and Victoria entertained them enthusiastically. She thought them both marvellous, but in her Journal she confessed that she liked Albert just a little better than his brother; she could hardly bear to say goodbye.

The day came, for which she was being prepared. King William IV died and Victoria, now eighteen, was "Her Majesty". She heard the news at dawn on a summer morning. Later that day she met her Councillors. Her small, upright figure, dressed in black; her serious, innocent face with its "Cupid's bow" mouth and large blue eyes; her grace of movement and the musical voice in which she read her first speech, impressed them all. She held out her hand for each one to kiss, as if she had been doing it for years.

The same day she ordered that her bed should be removed from her mother's room. Hitherto she had never been allowed a bedroom of her own. Now she was going to be independent.

King Leopold had advised her to make few political changes, so she asked Lord Melbourne, the elderly Prime Minister, to continue in office. His party, the Whigs, had reformed Parliament, though he was no reformer by nature and did not worry about social problems. With him beside her the young Queen was unlikely to do anything rash; she learned from him a great deal about her country's customs and the limits of what a sovereign can do. She found the business of governing not burdensome but intensely interesting under Melbourne's tuition: and for him it was a pleasure to discuss affairs with someone so fresh, unaffected and lively.

After her marriage to Prince Albert (1840) her education was not over. Albert was not yet called the Prince Consort; he was three months younger than the Queen. He had not parted from his own country and people without some regret, but was resolved to take full responsibility as though born of British stock. With unusual maturity and depth of character, he set himself to learn everything that could be useful and could help the Queen. Though in her eyes Albert was hardly less than perfect, he candidly told her when he saw her faults; and she gratefully tried to improve.

These five people, more than any others made Victoria what she was: her careful mother, her strict governess, her devoted uncle, her well-informed minister and her no less careful, strict, devoted, well-informed and affectionate husband.

2

Even if they had done nothing more adventurous than remain faithful to each other and raise a happy family, Victoria and Albert would have deserved gratitude from a nation whose Court life had been so long unsound—as has been said, one king mad, the next bad and the next a buffoon. But they took their public duties seriously and had no wish to remain blind to important happenings in the world.

The years 1840–50 were called the Hungry Forties (not that the twenties and thirties had been much better) because wages were very low and the Corn Laws kept bread prices high. Hunger reached its appalling peak in 1845–46 when the potato crop in Ireland failed and people died of starvation—"too terrible to think of," noted the Queen in her Journal, and promptly rationed her own household's bread supplies. After the Corn Laws were repealed the price of bread gradually came down. The fifties were less hungry, while the sixties, seventies and eighties saw a far higher standard of living for all except the extremely poor.

The decision in 1846 to import foreign corn and thus increase supplies and cheapen bread was taken by Sir Robert Peel, the next Prime Minister after Melbourne. Victoria had not liked Peel at first and grudged parting with her dear Melbourne, but as Peel's party (Conservative) had more seats in Parliament than Melbourne's, she accepted the unwritten law that the Sovereign appoints the leader of the major party rather than the person she would wish—and screwed herself up to have him. For his part, Peel had begun by upholding the Corn Laws and it needed courage to swing over to the opposite policy— Free Trade—of which most of his party thoroughly disapproved.

These were difficult decisions for both Queen and Minister, but neither let themselves be swayed by personal feelings. In the end she liked and trusted Peel as much as anyone. When he died, a picture appeared, called "Peel's Monument" *Punch*, 12 October, 1850. (Opposite.)

Poverty in Britain was still unconquered, but was equally bad in many cities abroad where despots still reigned, even after the French Revolution, and there was general discontent. In 1848 a small handbook for revolutionaries was published; plots ripened into action, barricades were built, bombs exploded and five European revolutions broke out. In London the Chartists, a society which wanted Votes for All, tried to hold a monster meeting on Clapham Common but, in pouring rain, it proved a failure. In Paris, however, amid tumult and uproar the French King abdicated; he took refuge with his wife in England.

Naturally Victoria was relieved that nothing worse had happened here. She was sure that her people "high and low, Lords and Shopkeepers" were setting an example of loyalty that would benefit other countries; England was and always would be the home of freedom, a land to which oppressed people or those expelled from their own lands could come.

Her husband held the same beliefs. He saw that this country which had pioneered the Industrial Revolution could lead others by producing not only consumable goods, but also an example of honest industry and civilised, harmonious living. He had a constant desire to promote peace between the peoples. With these ideas in mind he organised the Great Exhibition, which was held in a huge glass-house in Hyde Park —taking in some of the tall elm-trees there—in 1851.

The author of that revolutionary handbook, Karl Marx, was aiming at a "classless society", something which to Queen Victoria would have seemed very odd if she could have pictured it. To her, High and Low were like treble and bass; harmony required both, masters needed servants, and servants needed masters. In a snobbish age when high rank was worshipped as much as wealth, Victoria tended to shrink from the society of "the fashionables" and prefer the company of simple old countrywomen in their cottages, so far was she herself from being a snob.

Some of her happiest days when her nine children were growing up were the summers spent either in the Isle of Wight or the bracing air of Deeside. Victoria was keenly aware of beauty—as a girl she had loved ballet and opera—and in her rambles and rides was ready to be enchanted by a sunset or a "view". The Journal tells of a typical September day when she went to open a new bridge over the Dee (at that point a narrow stream), Albert wearing a plaid of Royal Stuart, "and I and the girls in skirts of the same", attended by their ladies who had only returned at five that morning from the Mar Lodge ball the night before; and how they were all met by the local gentry and a band, and drank "prosperity to the bridge" in whisky, after which they talked with the company, took tea and drove back to Balmoral, "home at half-past five, not without having some rain by the way".

Cynics in the twentieth century may scoff at Victoria's simple pleasures, but it remains true that in the sad years when the Prince was no longer at her side it soothed her spirit to watch the same clear water fleeting over the granite stones, and to lift her eyes to the same unchanging hills.

In 1857 Prince Albert was given the title of Prince Consort. He no longer merely heard now and then extracts which the Queen read to him from papers *she* had to deal with; he had long since been given the golden key which opened these boxes of papers, and the two discussed them and composed replies together.

Prince Albert's last public action before his death, when he was almost too weak to hold a pencil, was to insert alterations into a despatch about to be sent to the United States Government. Had the original sharp wording remained, it is thought likely that Britain and the U.S.A. would have gone to war with one another, but his suggestions were adopted and the atmosphere grew more friendly: it was a real stroke for peace.

The Prince was not robust and died from various causes, aged only forty-two. His widow could not and would not be comforted.

3

For three years after the Prince Consort's death Queen Victoria remained completely hidden from her people, and for many more years partially so. She continued her Journal, though it was long before she could bear to write down the entries for Prince Albert's last days. Meanwhile Liberal and Conservative governments alike (the old Whig and Tory names being dropped) produced useful Acts of Parliament marking progress in various ways. To these the royal assent was given while nobody outside the Palace saw the royal person.

France became once more an Empire under the great Napoleon's nephew, Napoleon III, who with his tall elegant Spanish wife Eugénie had once visited Victoria and Albert. The sixties were the time of their greatest splendour, when Paris was modernised and the Empress Eugénie set the fashions, but their Empire ended disastrously in 1871 and they fled to England with their son for refuge. Prussia, whose army had crushed France, became the leading State in a new political creation, the German Empire.

Victoria's feelings were painfully involved in these events—although Britain remained neutral—because of her friendship with the unfortunate Napoleon and Eugénie, but also because her eldest daughter was married to the Prussian who now became German Emperor. There were indeed few reigning families in Europe, imperial, royal or noble, with whom Victoria had not some family connection.

In another special way she could be regarded as the Head of a Family, for the world map was being covered more and more with dots and patches of red as Britain's Empire expanded. During her whole reign its area increased from just over 8, to just over 12 millions of square miles; its population from 96 million to 240 million men, women and children.

In 1877 the Conservative Prime Minister Disraeli suggested that Queen Victoria should take the title Empress of India, an idea to which she wholeheartedly responded. In the same year Britain took over a part of South Africa; four years later the Liberals led by Mr Gladstone gave it back to the Boers. This incident was not the only or most striking one in the "Grab for Africa", but it illustrates the opposite viewpoints of the two political parties and their rival spokesmen. In the excitement of the party struggle the Queen gradually came out of her retirement; 1875–85 has been called the most political period of her life.

The question on which parties disagreed most strongly was that of Home Rule for Ireland. Liberals thought Ireland should govern itself, Conservatives saw no reason to change the "Union". The Queen opposed Home Rule, but that was partly because she disliked Gladstone, "deluded old fanatic" (her words), and though she liked his wife she could not bring herself to express regret when after four Ministries totalling nearly 14 years he resigned. The Irish question was left unsettled.

Disraeli on the other hand could do nothing wrong in her eyes. She could not pretend to be impartial to these two men personally, but knew that as Queen she must be "above party"; obviously she found it very difficult.

The fiftieth anniversary of her accession was celebrated in 1887. She drove in an open carriage to Westminster Abbey for a Thanksgiving and the crowds saw her at last.

4

After Disraeli was dead and Gladstone retired, her Prime Ministers were either Lord Salisbury, bushy-bearded descendant of Queen Elizabeth's secretary Cecil, or for a brief while, the smooth-shaven Lord Rosebery, first chairman of the London County Council and leader of the Liberals. Lord Salisbury's knowledge of foreign affairs was formidable, and though he was neither so original nor so eloquent as Disraeli he ranks as one of the greatest of Conservative statesmen. Labour was represented by a few members in Victoria's later parliaments, but the party was not yet organised.

The Queen began to feel her age and unwillingly took to wearing silver-rimmed spectacles when she was indoors. Her Diamond Jubilee, the drive to St Paul's through six miles of deafening cheers from the madly excited crowds, she found exhausting, though it touched her deeply. The celebration was even more magnificent than that of ten years before and was attended by even more representatives of her Empire.

After that day of sunshine—"Queen's weather"—in June 1897, Victoria was still surprisingly active in public life. In the Boer War, which she much disliked but supposed *had* to be undertaken, few items of news from South Africa escaped her attention; an observer one day noticed her turning pale when a telegram was handed to her during lunch, for in the war's earlier stages the reports told of alarming failures and mistakes. She urged her government to send out two generals, Roberts and Kitchener, already tried and tested in various battlefields, and only when they arrived did Victoria's khaki-clad soldiers march to victory. Colonel Baden-Powell and his force, trapped in Mafeking, were relieved after a long siege, and the news, flashed by telegraph to England, was received in town and country with riotous joy, "people quite mad with delight", as she wrote in the Journal in May 1900.

Those yells and screams no doubt expressed pent-up feelings of relief, but something more; people felt confirmed in their belief that they always won in the end—that Britannia ruled the waves, that the Empire would go on for ever, and "God, Who made thee mighty, make thee mightier yet". Somehow the Queen seemed so much a part of this creed that the news of her death less than a year later seemed to many to knock the bottom out of their safe, comfortable world. But to many also, including millions who had never seen her, the old Queen's passing was like the parting from a deeply-loved Mother.

CHAPTER TWENTY-ONE

Edward VII: George V: Edward VIII

I

Unlike Prince Albert, who was keenly interested in the application of science to industry, Edward VII his son had no scientific bent. He described a submarine when he had been shown over it, as being "very complicated, and all of brass"—nothing more. As a boy he had been lazy at his lessons and quite indifferent to things that were "complicated". His parents had despaired at times.

But in Edward's reign research could safely be left to experts, and the Navy's top secrets were only known to a few. The naval yards and laboratories hummed with activity; submarines and battleships were being produced at high speed and in large numbers. Behind the ship-building programme lay the fear that Britain's naval power was threatened by that of the German Empire, and of this danger King Edward was well aware.

Edward's best stroke of statesmanship was that he did so much personally to bind Britain in friendship to France. He liked being in Paris and enjoyed its amusements, but he was a skilful diplomat as well and made effective the treaty of alliance called the Entente Cordiale in 1904.

In 1863 Edward had married the Danish Princess Alexandra. In her he had undoubtedly picked a winner—to use the racing language natural to this Turf-loving monarch, whose horses won the Derby three times. Alexandra won all hearts and the approval as well as affection of her mother-in-law Queen Victoria.

Whether as Princess of Wales or as Queen, the Danish lady was sympathetic to sufferers. She allowed the hospitals, which were then entirely kept up by voluntary giving, to call a day in June after her, Alexandra Day, when small artificial wild roses on pins were sold for hospital funds. Such was the origin of "flag days". Alexandra was gay and generous, and if she had a fault it was not a deadly one: she never could keep appointments in time and sometimes drove her husband frantic by her lateness for meals.

* This change of name was made according to the wish of H.M. King George V during the First World War.

130

PLATE XXVII   GEORGE V   *Oswald Birley*

PLATE XXVIII   *Sir John Lavery 1913*

THE ROYAL FAMILY AT BUCKINGHAM PALACE
(Detail)

PLATE XXIX   EDWARD VIII   *Frank Salisbury*
                                                            A pastel drawing

PLATE XXX   GEORGE VI   *Frank Beresford*

It is also pleasant to notice that their children loved them; between Edward VII and his son George (afterwards King) there existed a strong and lasting bond of affection.

2

More and more as the twentieth century unfolded, history points to happenings *in the reigns of* the monarchs, rather than events which *they* initiated or directed. Yet the personality of the kings cannot be disregarded. According to Edward VII's biographer (Sir Philip Magnus) a new pattern of monarchy had been created, which "made the Crown a rubber stamp politically, but enhanced . . . the force of its moral and emotional appeal"; and this pattern, he says, was triumphantly followed by all the successors of Queen Victoria.

For example, the most far-reaching, the most shattering event of George V's reign was the First World War. In 1914 the value of Edward VII's Entente Cordiale was tested and proved, as France and Britain remained inseparable allies. Then, the prompt spontaneous entry of Britain's self-governing Dominions into the war proved the solidarity of the Empire, a unity symbolised in the King as its Head. If further proof were needed that the Crown *meant* something, it could be found in the King's position as supreme commander of the fighting forces. "Your King and Country need you" said the recruiting posters; and young men flocked in their thousands to join the new armies.

George V never interfered with the conduct of operations, but expected to be kept informed (and kept himself informed by visits and inspections) how affairs were going. Never before were so many subjects in personal touch with their sovereign as during the war years, whether in ports, arsenals and industrial centres, or in hospitals or bombed areas. Five times he crossed over to France to get closer to the troops and see positions for himself. Like numerous other parents he and Queen Mary had a son serving out there—they also had one in the Navy. When food was scarce at home the royal household was rationed, and the King gave up alcoholic drinks to help people by his example to put their whole strength into the war effort. To be given any medal or title by such a man, so straight and simple, so selfless and hardworking, was felt to be truly an honour, something that recalled the early days of chivalry.

Besides expecting to be consulted and informed, a sovereign has the right to give warnings, advice or encouragement about anything that affects the Country's welfare. (In his diary or other writings George used to write "the Country" with a capital C.) He owed much to his wise secretary Lord Stamfordham, of whom he wrote: "the most loyal friend I ever had . . . he taught me how to be a king."

3

Earnest thought and effort was put by George V into seeking a solution to the Irish problem, which was specially acute after the Dublin street battles in Easter week 1916, in the midst of the other war. Murders, reprisals, ambushes, house-burnings, in short a reign of terror continued in many parts of the unhappy island for three years after the First World War had ended. But as the Irish patriot O'Connell had said, human blood is no cement for the temple of human liberty. A top-level Conference was summoned in 1921 between leaders of Britain, Ulster and the rest of Ireland to work out terms of peace. The agonising question was, would Mr De Valera, President of the illegal organisation that had been set up in Dublin, consent to attend it.

That he did so, was largely due to the King, who was dissatisfied with the Note which his Cabinet proposed to send to the Irish leader, as he considered it too abrupt, too threatening. By his wish a new Note was prepared, "the conciliatory tone of which was in marked contrast to the aggressive tone of the original one".* On receiving it, De Valera agreed to come. The Conference, after nearly two months, reached the settlement by which Ireland, except for Ulster which remained part of the United Kingdom, became a self-governing Dominion.

This arrangement was not final, for Eire gradually cut all the legal ties with Britain and in 1937 became a Republic; but the positive gain— the miracle, some might have said—was the atmosphere in which any agreement at all *could* be made, by men talking round a table and not at the point of a gun.

George V knew well that the difficulties between Britain and Ireland after seven hundred years were not going to disappear overnight, but at the first opening of the Ulster Parliament—which he attended in person—he had expressed his faith in the future. He ended his speech by saying, "May this historic gathering be the prelude of the day in which the Irish people, north and south . . . shall work together in common love for Ireland upon the sure foundation of mutual justice and respect."

* See Harold Nicolson, *King George V*, p. 359.

Changes in the status of all the Dominions was legalised by the Statute of Westminster (1931). These countries were now to be independent though freely associated with Britain in the Commonwealth and united by common allegiance to the Crown.

4

Two sons of George V and Queen Mary played their parts in the First World War: the elder one in the Grenadier Guards, the younger in H.M.S. *Collingwood*. These two came next in the long line of kings.

When the war ended, Edward the Prince of Wales was free to travel. He used his time touring the Dominions, the U.S.A. and India. Wherever he went he was rapturously received, except in some places in India where the crowds were silent—only, however, because Britain's relationship with India was then at about its worst; the Prince's tact and personal courage were admitted by all.

On the death of George V, who was sincerely mourned, Edward VIII was very generally welcomed by the Empire or as it was now more often called, the Commonwealth. He had only reigned for ten months when an unusual crisis occurred. He wished to marry Mrs Simpson, an American lady who was about to divorce her second husband; but would she be acceptable as Queen? Various opinions were asked and the reply given through the Prime Minister was, that none of the King's subjects would regard this lady as one who could share with him the responsibilities of the throne. Sooner than give her up, Edward decided to give up his kingship. He abdicated in favour of his next brother, who was already happily and suitably married, and the father of two little girls.

These words were spoken by the new King to his Councillors directly after his accession:

Your Royal Highnesses, My Lords and Gentlemen,

I meet you today in circumstances which are without parallel in the history of our Country. Now that the duties of Sovereignty have fallen to me, I declare to you my adherence to the strict principles of constitutional government and my resolve to work before all else for the welfare of the British Commonwealth of Nations.

With my Wife as helpmeet by my side, I take up the heavy task which lies before me. In it I look for the support of all my peoples.

He then said that he would confer a dukedom on his elder brother, who would henceforth be known as H.R.H the Duke of Windsor.

CHAPTER TWENTY-TWO

George VI

I

The second son of George V had been christened Albert and was known as Bertie in his family, but now took the title of George VI. He resembled his father in various ways. Neither of them had expected to become king, but whereas George V's elder brother had died in 1892, which gave him a long time to prepare for kingship, George VI had to face it suddenly in the few days before his brother's abdication.

Both Georges began their career in the Navy. George VI started as a twelve-year-old cadet and served for nine years, but his health was uncertain and in 1917 it was decided that he was no longer physically fit for service at sea. (Later, he was able to serve in the Royal Air Force.)

Then, in 1914 and 1939, both kings had to lead a nation at war. Among many points of comparison between the First World War and the Second, one striking difference was the larger share taken in the latter by civilians—not willingly, but having it thrust upon them. The enemy's air-power and submarines were aimed at breaking down the resistance of the islanders, who thus had to face all the possibilities of death and destruction from the air, starvation by the loss of their shipping and invasion of their land by enemy forces.

In other words, the war was total. Therefore the importance of strong, selfless character in men and women of every degree could not be over-estimated. Without question, the way George VI and Queen Elizabeth lived from start to finish was a war-winning factor. They stayed mainly in London, though at times they used to sleep at Windsor where the princesses were, and travel to London by day. They saw whole streets in the East End laid flat, and talked to rescue-workers and survivors. They visited all the badly bombed cities. Buckingham Palace itself was hit altogether nine times; the King's study was wrecked when he luckily was not in it and all along one side of the palace the windows were shattered. Nothing turned the royal pair away from the work they had to do, and nothing shook their belief that finally the just cause would win. No one can measure how much their example united and encouraged their people.

During the pause between the first Allied victory in North Africa, and the later attack on Sicily, George VI flew over to Algiers (June 1943). Five hundred young British soldiers bathing in the Mediterranean suddenly saw their King appear on the sun-scorched beach. They swarmed around him singing "For he's a jolly good fellow" just as the boys had done in pre-war camps which, when Duke of York, he had organised in Suffolk.

"Down the road," wrote one lad in a desert outpost shortly after this, in a letter to his mother, "came a big open Ford V8 flying the Royal Standard. It passed us quite slowly and there, nodding to the crowd, was the King himself in the uniform of a Field Marshal. We felt then that we were not quite so far from home." About the meaning of British monarchy, that last sentence can reveal nearly as much as a whole lecture on the Constitution.

The North African tour, lasting a fortnight in which the King covered 6,700 miles, was a time both exhausting and rewarding. Before his return to England he spent an unforgettable day at Malta, whose people had endured fifteen months of bombardment and hunger —the island which as an island had been uniquely awarded the George Cross for its gallantry.

At each Christmas as the war went on, King George spoke to his people over the air, like his father before him. Such high moments as that of the ending of hostilities also called for a broadcast. He never enjoyed speech-making, as he had been troubled since childhood with a stammer, but since beginning treatment with an Australian speech-therapist (Mr Logue) he had definitely improved, and never lost his determination to conquer the defect; latterly it was hardly noticeable. His voice became as well known as that of his great Prime Minister Churchill. At these times the King showed a rare gift for expressing, with simplicity and depth, the spiritual values held in common by the free nations.

2

Not surprisingly, the handwriting of George VI was similar to that of his father, indeed the signature "G.R.I." of George V (R.I. stood for Rex Imperator or King Emperor) was said to be indistinguishable from the "G.R.I." of his son. But after 1947 George VI was signing his papers "G.R." only. The letter "I" was dropped. In this seemingly small detail was packed a most potent chapter of history.

George VI, who had never been to India, found himself at his accession Emperor of a vast sub-continent peopled with different races, using over six hundred languages, all under British overlordship direct or indirect, some of the lands still being ruled by their own Princes. Queen Victoria had promised that all should freely practise their own religion; later Reports had recommended that Indians be associated with British officials in governing. The latter change was only taking place very slowly as the British administrators, who were undoubtedly efficient, kept apart from the "natives" and thought them in general not efficient enough. Meanwhile the Indian National Congress had been formed and was claiming Home Rule for India.

The Mahatma (= holy man) Mohundas Gandhi worked for many years to prepare Indians for the time when they would rule themselves. The British connection, he thought, had made India more helpless than ever before, and it was sinful to serve the British government. For such sayings Gandhi had been imprisoned, but would not let his followers use firearms or act as rebels; they were to use *Satya-graha*. This word implies not so much a method as a way of life. *Satya* means "truth", and *graha* means "force", but to translate truth-force as "non-violence" makes it sound pale and negative, whereas it meant something passionate—the power of truth and rightness within a man, acting in obedience to what Gandhi called the inner voice. This was the dynamic that finally altered India's status and situation. "India," said Gandhi, "stands in awe of power and wealth. But it loves the humble servant of the poor. Possessions, elephants, jewels, armies, palaces, win India's obedience. Sacrifice and renunciation win its heart."

Gandhi, then, whose finger touched the pulse of millions, longed for freedom through a friendly understanding with Britain—not, he said, "an imperialistic haughty Britain", but one "humbly trying to serve the common end of humanity".

By 1945 Britain was ready to make India a Dominion on the pattern of Canada. The chief obstacle was that the Hindu majority and Moslem minority of the people would not mix, nor leave each other alone. There had been constant riots with bloodshed. Gandhi begged Moslems and Hindus to stop them, and co-operate; but in vain. The British authorities did all they could. The Viceroy (Lord Wavell) brought the Hindu leader (Mr Nehru) and the Moslem leader (Mr Jinnah) to London. King George VI had them both to lunch and sat between the two men who represented such powerful antagonisms. All efforts at peace-making were useless.

Nevertheless the new arrangements went forward. In the end, not a Dominion but two separate States were set up—India for the Hindus, and a Moslem State geographically divided into two blocks east and west, called Pakistan. The Viceroy appointed to bring British rule to an end and hand over, was Lord Mountbatten, King George's cousin. (Both were Queen Victoria's great-grandsons.) He ably performed his difficult task.

Still the hate-filled fanatics of the two religions went on slaughtering one another. Gandhi, who felt each violent act like a sword-thrust in his own body, undertook to fast for Moslem–Hindu unity and peace. He was now in his seventy-ninth year. He touched no food or drink for five days—though this was not his longest fast; he had once done it for three weeks.

Later in the same month (January 1948) the Mahatma was shot dead by a Hindu fanatic. Shocking and tragic as his death was, Gandhi's life-work was done.

*　　*　　*

This all too brief sketch of the close of Britain's "Indian Empire" explains why the King left out "I" when signing his papers; it may also suggest why a man like George VI felt inadequate in face of the vast, intricate, stubborn problem which his Empire had become. That lunch-party with Mr Nehru and Mr Jinnah seemed to be on one of those blank days that everybody knows, when one has the feeling of having got nowhere. King George, rather depressed, wrote in his diary that one of the Indian statesmen had talked a great deal, the other hardly at all; while he himself had prepared a few words to say, but feeling that the moment was unfavourable, had not said them!

Yet his patience and goodwill never faltered—the wish to understand, to be of use, to reconcile, to serve, was undefeated. This Rex, Imperator or not, never spared himself trouble, nor did he ever take the easy way out, or look for popularity, or give up in despair.

3

George VI and Queen Elizabeth visited the U.S.A. and Canada just before the Second World War. He was the first reigning British sovereign to set foot on American soil.

After that came the War and distant travelling was impossible. In 1947 they went out to South Africa, taking the two Princesses Elizabeth and Margaret with them. They all enjoyed going together as a family. The people of the Union as well as Zululand, Bechuanaland, Basutoland and Southern Rhodesia gave them overwhelming welcome, while in the words of George's biographer "the great pageant of the African scene which unrolled before them held them fascinated and spellbound".

During this tour Princess Elizabeth had her twenty-first birthday, and she broadcast a message to all the Commonwealth peoples. It was quite spontaneous, but must have given her father deep satisfaction, for it showed she had made her own that same desire to reconcile and to serve. (An American observer who saw her later on, in Washington, remarked on her quiet strength and serenity: "this cannot all be trained into her, there is something deeper, God-given, I believe.")

Later in 1947 she was married to Lieutenant Philip Mountbatten, R.N. (Prince Philip of Greece) who was given the title of H.R.H. The Duke of Edinburgh.

The King and Queen celebrated their own Silver Wedding in 1948 and were planning a tour in Australia and New Zealand for 1949, but this had to be postponed and was later cancelled on medical advice.

The King's state of health caused some anxiety over the next few years; however after treatment and two operations his strength seemed to have returned and the winter months of 1951–52 passed normally. Christmas was spent as usual at Sandringham, the Norfolk country house which George VI specially loved—again like his father. By now he had two little grand-children, Prince Charles and Princess Anne; once more the whole royal family were together.

He had accepted for the Queen and himself an invitation from the South African government to go there and enjoy the sunny climate for a few weeks, as private guests. They were to set off early in March 1952. About a month before that, on February 6th at Sandringham, he passed away peacefully in his sleep. His age was fifty-six.

4

In the half-darkness and raw cold of a February morning, people could be seen standing four deep all along the Thames Embankment from the House of Lords to Lambeth Bridge. Some had been there all

PLATE XXXI

Herbert James Gunn 1950

CONVERSATION PIECE AT THE ROYAL LODGE, WINDSOR

PLATE XXXII   ELIZABETH II   *Pietro Annigoni*

night. As Big Ben chimed eight the doors of Westminster Hall opened, and the front of the queue silently moved forward.

Within, four Guardsmen with rifles reversed stood, absolutely still, at the corners of a catafalque draped in purple and covered with the Union Jack. One by one, men and women passed slowly by the coffin where their King's body lay at rest. Footsteps made a slight shuffling noise on the stone floor; dim and far off sounded the traffic hum of London.

Tall candles were burning, but lit the scene only faintly, and the high roof was in darkness. Up there, hidden at that moment, were beautifully carved beams fashioned by medieval craftsmen from oak that was once living wood—trees whose roots were deep in Sussex soil before the Normans came. Here was the very place where Richard II had listened to the causes of his people's discontent. Here he had handed over to Bolingbroke the tokens of his sovereignty, and gone forth a prisoner.

In this place of memories, too, another king had been tried and found wanting. All his Stuart dignity and charm could not save the man who was solemnly judged to have broken the contract between sovereign and people.

And now—the contrast! Dull would he be indeed of soul who could pass by—unmoved—"a sight so touching in its majesty".

It only took a minute to walk from one door to the other. So the citizens moved on and were soon out in the open air again, to disperse and to begin their day's work. If those passers-by could have put into words what they felt, it might have been something like this:

"We liked you, King George. You were one of us. You had a tough job, not of your asking, and you did it darned well. We're grateful. We could do with more high-ups like you."

Meanwhile the nearness of the Abbey across the road with Edward the Confessor's shrine within it, was a reminder that when a man takes up the burden of kingship and wears the Crown he is set apart, touched by the grace of God, and "hallowed" to be king.

CHAPTER TWENTY-THREE

Elizabeth II

I

When Elizabeth II ascended the throne, her people sensed that the coming reign held great promise. Remembering Elizabeth I and Victoria, they believed that a queen would again lead and inspire the nation. As a princess, she had already won widespread affection.

On her twenty-first birthday she had dedicated herself to her future subjects in these words:

"I declare before you all that my whole life, whether it be long or short, shall be devoted to your service, and the service of our great Imperial family to which we all belong. But," she added, "I shall not have the strength to carry out this resolution alone unless you join in it with me, as I now invite you to do. I know that your support will be unfailingly given."

She has fulfilled her vow and reigns with grace and distinction. As well as carrying one of the most arduous jobs in the world, the Queen now has four children: Charles, Anne, Andrew born in 1960 and Edward in 1964.

Time slips away quickly, and the Queen spoke of her surprise to find, early in 1972, that the twenty-fifth anniversary of her wedding to the Duke of Edinburgh was so close at hand. Two and a half decades of married life had passed, and twenty years of her reign.

Indefatigably the Queen and her husband have travelled, seeing the Commonwealth and other countries, where their talks with responsible people have given them a wide, perhaps unique, knowledge of world affairs. But nobody can claim that these years have been smooth sailing, either at home or abroad.

Despite improved living conditions at home for many, crime has increased and a minority of Her Majesty's subjects, far from helping her to keep that youthful vow, seem unable or unwilling to halt the downward drag from civilisation to barbarism. Yet in an age when liberty is so often confused with licence, it has meant much to have at the core of the nation's life one genuinely united family.

"We all know," said the Queen to London's Lord Mayor at her Silver Wedding banquet, "about the difficulties of achieving that 'happy family' of which you have spoken. But if it succeeds, there is nothing like it. . . . When the Bishop was asked what he thought about sin he replied with simple conviction that he was against it. If I am asked today what I think about family life after twenty-five years of marriage I can answer with equal simplicity and conviction, 'I am for it'."

She further emphasised that no marriage can hope to succeed without a deliberate attempt to be tolerant and understanding. 'This doesn't come easily to individuals and it certainly doesn't come naturally to communities and nations. A civilised and peaceful existence is only possible when people make the effort to understand each other. Looking at the world, one might be forgiven for believing that many people have never heard of this simple idea. . . ."

2

The children of the Queen and Prince Philip are certainly not conventional copies of their parents. The two elder ones have shown strongly individual traits and are already well-known in public life.

After his years of study at Cambridge and Aberystwyth and a period in the Royal Air Force, Prince Charles entered the Royal Navy, which by his parents' choice and his own, is to be his professional career. In 1969 he was ceremonially invested as Prince of Wales at the ancient castle of Caernarvon, and perhaps more thoroughly than any royal heir before him, has identified himself with the people and traditions of the Principality. His mastery of the Welsh language proved his desire to do so, as well as his capacity for hard work.

The same enthusiasm and thoroughness have marked Princess Anne's progress in her chosen field as she has grown through the years—from a saddle-happy little girl such as might be met with in any pony club to the brilliant performer, a magnet for every eye at equestrian events, and winner of many trophies. The best school education ever devised is unlikely to develop this quality, this determination to master difficulties, unless there is also backing and, above all, example from a young person's parents.

Awkward moments there have been, when the natural eagerness of the people to see their sovereign and "the royals" has overflowed into inquisitiveness, and photographers have become too pressing. But, generally, good manners have prevailed and in recent years the Queen has "walked about" increasingly often in crowded streets, as informally as she does among invited guests in her own garden.

3

"The Queen has an interesting face," commented Pietro Annigoni, painter of the portrait reproduced on p. 144. "The face is radiant when she smiles or talks, but when she is thinking or concentrating she almost looks like another person."

Though never directly involved in party politics, the sovereign is no mere spectator; she receives reports from her Ministers, discusses, advises, and speaks her mind. Throughout the troubles in Northern Ireland her public utterances, never lacking in discretion, made it clear how realistically and sensitively she bore that burden; and wherever there is mass suffering, whether due to man's lawlessness or nature's upheavals, none can better voice a nation's sorrow and sympathy.

1972 was not only a milestone in the Queen's personal life. Long negotiations and debates culminated in Britain's application to join the European Economic Community and to become a full member in 1973: a decision which many feared would break up the Commonwealth.

The Queen has never wavered in her belief that the British Commonwealth is meant to be, and is, a global force making for stability and peace: a living proof that with goodwill a multi-racial society is viable in the modern world. In her Christmas message just before New Year's Day 1973 she said:

"The new links with Europe will not replace those with the Commonwealth. They cannot alter our historical and personal attachments with kinsmen and friends overseas. Old friends will not be lost; Britain will take her Commonwealth links into Europe with her."

Here the story of England's sovereigns, traced in this book through nine centuries and more, reaches the present day, with many future pages yet to be written. "What infinite heart's ease must kings neglect, that private men enjoy!" Elizabeth of twentieth-century England could well echo those words of Shakespeare's Henry the Fifth, though he follows them with a long diatribe against ceremony, and she knows full well that ceremonial is something her people love. Long may she reign, with or without ceremony, free to enjoy fully all the heart's ease her position can allow.

Royal Portraiture

by RICHARD ORMOND

Assistant Keeper, National Portrait Gallery

In the past, royal portraiture has played a more important part than merely recording the likeness of a particular individual for posterity. A royal portrait was the image of kingly virtue and majesty, remote, formal and often awe-inspiring. This was particularly the case when a king was shown in an impressive architectural setting, like Henry VIII in Holbein's wall-painting at Whitehall Palace (destroyed by fire in 1698), or Charles I apparently riding down one of the corridors of St James's Palace in Van Dyck's great equestrian portrait of him. Before the days of photography and other mass media, portraiture provided the only means of propagating the royal image, and impressing subjects with the tangible presence of royal power. It is not surprising, therefore, that a great many royal portraits have survived, many of them copies or versions after a successful prototype. The demand for them was large, and they were widely dispersed; on diplomatic and marriage missions abroad, to local institutions, courtiers and loyal subjects. In some cases, successful court painters literally set up factories in order to turn out the enormous number of replicas required, particularly Lely, Kneller and their successors. The function of royal portraits as a means of propaganda can perhaps be exaggerated, but it is clear that they were intended to enhance the dignity and authority of kingship. Hence the imposing settings, the formal poses, the elaborate clothes and insignia of office and the general atmosphere of pomp and circumstance. A court portraitist was not called upon to paint an intimate or revealing portrait of his patron, but to present him in the best possible light.

English portraiture before the sixteenth century is extremely limited. The medieval mind was not primarily interested in the individual, and had little desire to render the physical reality of the world or its inhabitants. The images of early kings, whether on stained glass (as Edward the Confessor, p. 13), illuminated manuscript, coin or tomb are the formal emblems of royal status, and are not really recognisable likenesses at all. They are stiff, hierarchical and characterless. Our medieval kings lie frozen in state, with rigid features, encased in robes of state, or armour (as Richard I, p. 30 and Henry III, p. 36). Yet it would be untrue to say that there are no painted portraits of early kings. Richard II, civilised, sophisticated and clearly in advance of his time, is represented by two paintings, the impressive whole-length portrait of him in Westminster Abbey, a copy of which is reproduced here (Plate I), and the famous Wilton diptych in the National Gallery, as well as a tomb effigy, also in Westminster Abbey. The face in all these likenesses is immediately recognisable, thin and delicate, with a long, pointed nose. Portraiture in terms of rendering the features of a particular individual has begun, in however stylised and primitive a fashion.

The two portraits of Richard II are unique for their time, for they were either painted during his reign or soon after. Surviving portraits of fifteenth-century kings were painted in the sixteenth century presumably, but not certainly, after lost originals, which have not survived. In one instance, that of Henry IV (Plate II), the likeness is definitely false, being derived from the portrait of a French king. The popularity of sets of royal portraits clearly tempted someone to fill the gap, in this case at the cost of accuracy. Compared with continental examples these early portraits are wooden and lifeless to a degree. Even so, the portrait of Richard III (Plate VI) is a refreshing antidote to the hunch-backed villain of Shakespeare's play and Tudor propaganda in general. He looks considerably more humane and honest than his rival Henry VII, whose portrait (Plate VII) suggests cunning and unscrupulousness. This portrait of Henry VII is, however, much more vivid and realistic than anything which had been painted up to that time, showing Henry leaning his hands on the edge of the frame itself, holding a red rose— the symbol of his dynasty. It is attributed to the Austrian painter, Michael Sittium, who accompanied Herman Rincke on an embassy from Isabella of Austria with a marriage proposal. Such portraits, in the days of dynastic alliances, were the only means of seeing your prospective partner before marriage, and served an important function. Henry VIII, who had only seen Holbein's portrait of Anne of Cleves before he married her, was extremely disappointed with his new wife in person, and scornfully referred to her as the "Flanders Mare".

There was nothing in the history of English portraiture to prepare for the advent of Holbein in 1525. A master of the High Rennaissance, he brought with him a mature, continental style with which he was to create an enduring image of Henry VIII and his court. When we think of Henry VIII, it is Holbein's Henry VIII that we see, with his large head, massive frame, broad shoulders and legs confidently astride. No wonder that those who entered the Privy Chamber at Whitehall Palace, and saw Henry's imposing figure looking down on them from the walls, felt that they were in the presence of no ordinary monarch, but one with unlimited power and authority. Even in the small and intimate panel portrait of him, a copy of which is reproduced here (Plate VIII), painted as a pair to the portrait of his third wife, Jane Seymour, soon after they were married, Henry's personality is overwhelming. The effect is vividly realistic and three-dimensional, quite unlike the stiff and primitive portraits of earlier kings. Although Holbein did not found a flourishing native school of art, he did have one or two immediate followers of some interest, like the painter of the portrait of Edward VI (Plate IX), based on a drawing by Holbein himself, and the painter of the imposing full-length of Lady Jane Grey (Plate X), depicted here as a grand court lady, rather than the frail and innocent victim of her father-in-law's intrigue. Previously thought to be a portrait of Katherine Parr, Henry's last wife, it has only recently been identified as Lady Jane Grey on the evidence of the huge jewel at her breast, which also appears in the earliest authentic engraving of her.

During the Elizabethan age portraiture becomes increasingly formalised, and the influence of Holbein disappears. Clothes, coats of arms and the emblems of position and office become more important than individual characterisation. This rigidity and lack of range in the fine arts is in striking contrast to the other achievements of the period, particularly in literature. The mask-like quality of many Elizabethan portraits may partly be due to the influence of Elizabeth herself, who became hypersensitive about her looks as she grew older, and only allowed her face to be painted after certain youthful patterns. The mask in her case was a protection against the ravages of time. The portrait of her painted in 1592 to commemorate her visit to the home of Sir Henry Lee at Ditchley in Oxfordshire is profoundly impressive (Plate XII). Elizabeth stands on a map of Southern England, dressed in a fantastically ornate robe (clothes were her one extravagance), her virtues expounded in a poem beside her. The picture is a blend of allegory and idealisation so typical of the age, but how tenuous and abstract

Elizabeth herself appears in comparison with Holbein's rendering of Henry VIII. Her portrait bears little relation to contemporary accounts of her old and wizened appearance.

During the Jacobean age portraiture becomes increasingly naturalistic and three-dimensional, chiefly due to the influence of Dutch and Flemish art. The human being emerges from behind his mask, his body again assumes a tangible form. James I (Plate XIII) is not, like Elizabeth in the Ditchley portrait, an imposing deity, but a tired, old man, weighed down by his Garter Robes and the cares of office. The culmination of this trend towards greater naturalism is Van Dyck, one of the greatest European portraitists of the seventeenth century, and a master of the Baroque. Like Holbein at the court of Henry VIII, Van Dyck at the court of Charles I created an enduring image of the Royalists, helping to perpetrate the legend of their doomed but romantic cause. His portraits have a breath-taking virtuosity, a sense of scale and vivid actuality, combined with a sensitive quality of melancholy and intelligence. This is most apparent in the portraits of Charles himself, as for example in the great equestrian portrait at the National Gallery. Charles rides out of a wood on a huge charger, a slight but imperious figure, who is, in this extraordinarily beautiful setting, both withdrawn and rather sad, and still enormously dignified. The same is true of Van Dyck's portrait of him in armour, a copy of which is reproduced here (Plate XIV), where his long, cultivated face emphasises the distinction of the figure and setting.

The influence of Van Dyck on his successors can clearly be seen by comparing the portrait of Charles with that of William III after Lely (Plate XVII), where the pose and armour are almost identical, or with the portrait of James II (Plate XVI) possibly by Gennari. It is dangerous to compare kings on the evidence of their portraits, but the apparent pride and flamboyance of James II contrast strongly with the common-sense and caution of his successor. Van Dyck's influence was not confined to male portraiture, for it is evident, in a rather coarse and undistinguished form, in the portrait of Mary after Wissing (Plate XI). Mary's dress may seem to be daringly and unsuitably decolleté, and the pose a little undignified for a state portrait, but such things were an expression of the easy conventions and conceits of post-Cromwellian England. The dull portrait of Anne (Plate XIX) is a return to a more formal and reticent tradition.

English art was only finally freed from its dependence on European art and foreign artists, like Lely and Kneller, by the native genius of Hogarth. His influence seems apparent in the amusing and characterful portrait of George II by Worlidge (Plate XXI), which is almost a caricature. It is a welcome change, however, from the bland portraiture of Kneller ("a lot of wigs with Whigs inside them"), like his portrait of George I, a version of which is reproduced here (Plate XX). In the main, the great names of eighteenth-century English art were not employed by the court, but there were several competent painters who were. One of these, Allan Ramsay, painted a most successful portrait of George III (studio version see Plate XXII), his handsome face and energetic pose evenly matched with his State Robes and the luxuriant draperies behind. One tends to think of George III as an old man, slowly going mad, and forgets that he ascended the throne at the age of twenty-two. George IV was more fortunate than his father in having a court portraitist admirably suited to his personality and the Regency period as a whole. Sir Thomas Lawrence was a painter of European significance, trained in the formal traditions of the eighteenth century, but with an impassioned brush and glowing colour-sense that proclaimed his romantic sympathies. His portraits have enormous zest and life, and if at times they cater to the vulgar and sentimental qualities of the age, they are never dull. His unfinished sketch of George IV (Plate XXIII) is remarkably lively and successful, as indeed is the full-length state portrait at Windsor Castle.

Lawrence's influence was paramount in the early part of the nineteenth century, becoming slowly more domesticated and restrained, as shown in the mediocre portrait of William IV by an unknown artist (Plate XXIV). Queen Victoria, ascending the throne as an attractive young girl, was a refreshing change from her two elderly and unprepossessing uncles. Hayter's idealised portrait of her in Coronation Robes, carrying the panoply of state with youthful dignity, her innocent face beatifically gazing upwards, reflects the upsurge of patriotic emotion with which her reign was greeted (Plate XXV). She seemed to embody all the hopes of a new age, where England was to be the greatest power in the world, its moral and intellectual leader as well. Later portraits of Victoria, of which there are a great many, emphasise other aspects of her personality and position. With the decay of royal power she became a symbol of national pride, a beloved figurehead, whose life and attitudes epitomised the Victorian age. Newspapers and journals demanded a more informal and human image of her than would have been possible in earlier centuries, and her small, stout figure became a familiar feature of the age. The royal portrait as an agent of propaganda was no longer necessary. Nevertheless, there was still room for state portraits to commemorate special occasions, like Fildes' Coronation portrait of Edward VII, a replica of which is reproduced here (Plate XXVI).

Portraiture in the twentieth century has always seemed something of an anachronism. This is partly due to the fact that portraiture has largely been superseded by the camera, but also because few modern artists of any quality have been interested in the visible world at all. The kind of psychological revelation which certain modern portraits display is obviously unsuitable for the portrayal of royalty. Modern royal portraits, therefore, tend to be rather tame and conventional, relying on well-worn methods of style and composition. They convey a likeness, but little else. In the modern world the demand for grand portraits, even of kings, is a demand of habit and tradition, which is often at variance with the more creative developments of modern art. Henry VIII no longer needs to impress upon us the majesty and power of royal authority.

BIBLIOGRAPHY

The sources for this book have been mainly the standard histories of England and the *Dictionary of National Biography*.

The following is a short list of recommended books, most of which carry extensive bibliographies of their own subject and period:

Life of King Edward the Confessor, ed. R. Barlow (Nelson's Medieval Texts)

Dean Stanley: *Memorials of Westminster Abbey* (Murray)

John Appleby: *Henry II* (Bell)

E. M. Routh: *Lady Margaret* (O.U.P.)

Garrett Mattingly: *The Defeat of the Spanish Armada* (Cape)

C. V. Wedgwood: *The Trial of Charles I* (Collins)

Frank A. Mumby: *George III and the American Revolution* (Constable)

Elizabeth Longford: *Victoria R.I.* (Weidenfeld and Nicolson)

J. W. Wheeler-Bennett: *George VI. His Life and Reign* (Macmillan)

INDEX

For quick reference, personal names are distinguished from non-personal
(places, etc.); the latter are indented.